Do Angels Wear Overalls?

What Others are Saying...

Wow! Here are amazing stories about our amazing God. I laughed, I cried, and gave thanks as I read. You will also! Throughout these pages the work of God is highlighted, sometimes clearly showing Himself in a miracle while at other times "behind the scenes" to accomplish His plan through ordinary people. In a world filled with constant bad news, these real-life adventures inspire the heart and strengthen faith. God is still at work. Read and worship! Read and pray! Read and be encouraged!

DR. DON BADER
Intercultural Ministries
AG U.S. Missions

"Do Angels Wear Overalls?" That may seem a strange question until you have read this incredible account of the work and ministries two very dear and lifelong friends, Bill and Hilda Bradney, whose poured-out lives of faithful obedience to God's call have resulted in countless thousands of lost souls being brought into the kingdom of God and the church of Jesus Christ advanced throughout the world. Their riveting accounts of miracles of New Testament proportion in their own lives and the lives of others will also encourage you to believe for yourself and those you love that "the same Lord over all is rich unto all who call upon Him" (Romans 10:12b KJV).

And one more thing—I predict that once you have started to read this powerful book you won't be able to put it down until you have read the last page! Thank you Bill and Hilda for lives so well lived to the glory of God! May Jesus Christ be praised!

DONALD G. KROAH, D.MIN.

Senior Pastor, Plymouth Haven Baptist Church
Alexandria, VA
Host, The Don Kroah Show
WAVA Radio, Washington, DC
Founder & President, Reach Africa Now, Inc.

Evie and I loved reading these 48 windows into the amazing journey of faith of missionaries Bill and Hilda Bradney. Within these stories the reader is given a behind the scenes look into the remarkable lives of these two choice servants of God. We have always said that to know the Bradney's is to love and admire them; but even beyond their part in the stories is the inspiring testimony of the faithfulness of God in their lives. We commend this book to you with highest recommendations.

DR. DON MEYER

Former President of University of Valley Forge
Phoenixville, PA

Author Hilda Bradney's sister and brother-in-law Pauline and Halden Curtiss pastored Little Brown Church in Bigfork, MT, in the late 1960s, where my in-laws Jerry and Shirley Windle came to Christ as a young married couple, were discipled, and went to the mission field. My own first memories as preschool daughter of missionaries to Latin America was Costa Rica where Hilda and Bill Bradney served many years. So it was a great joy to meet and discover past connections over the production of this book *Do*

Angels Wear Overalls? Beyond a captivating story of the Bradney's missionary career, the amazing accounts of divine intervention in this book are a reminder that in a world of much turmoil and trial, faith still does move mountains and God's purposes will always prevail. I cannot recommend this book strongly enough.

JEANETTE WINDLE

missions journalist
editor BCM World Magazine
missionary BCM International
author *All Saints, Forgiven*, and
Hope Underground: The Chilean Mine Rescue

Do Angels Wear Overalls?

And More Stories of Divine Intervention from a Missionary Life

By: Hilda Bradney

Bradney Publications

Copyright Hilda Bradney © 2022
All rights reserved

All rights reserved. No part of this book shall be reproduced or transmitted in any form or by any means, electronic, mechanical, magnetic, photographic including photocopying, recording or by any information storage and retrieval system, without prior written permission of the publisher. No patent liability is assumed with respect to the use of the information contained herein. Although every precaution has been taken in the preparation of this book, the publisher and author assume no responsibility for errors or omissions. Neither is any liability assumed for damages resulting from the use of the information contained herein.

Scriptures marked AMP are taken from the AMPLIFIED BIBLE (AMP). Copyright © 1954, 1958, 1962, 1964, 1965, 1987 by the Lockman Foundation Used by Permission.

Scriptures marked ESV are taken from the THE HOLY BIBLE, ENGLISH STANDARD VERSION (ESV). Copyright© 2001 by Crossway, a publishing ministry of Good News Publishers. Used by permission.

Scriptures marked KJV are taken from the KING JAMES VERSION (KJV). Public domain.

Scriptures marked NIV are taken from THE HOLY BIBLE, NEW INTERNATIONAL VERSION. Copyright© 1973, 1978, 1984, 2011 by Biblica, Inc.™. Used by permission of Zondervan.

Scriptures marked NKJV are taken from the NEW KING JAMES VERSION (NKJV). Copyright© 1982 by Thomas Nelson, Inc. Used by permission. All rights reserved.

Scriptures marked NLT are taken from the HOLY BIBLE, NEW LIVING TRANSLATION. Copyright©1996, 2004, 2007 by Tyndale House Foundation. Used by permission of Tyndale House Publishers, Inc., Carol Stream, Illinois 60188. All rights reserved. Used by permission.

Scriptures marked NLV are taken from the THE HOLY BIBLE, NEW LIFE VERSION (NLV). Copyright© 1986 by Barbour Publishing. Used by permission.

Scriptures marked TLB are taken from the THE LIVING BIBLE (TLB). Copyright© 1971. Used by permission of Tyndale House Publishers, Inc., Carol Stream, Illinois 60188. All rights reserved.

Bradney Publications

Published by Bradney Publications.

ISBN print version 978-0-578-38067-4

ISBN electronic version 979-8-9865312-0-5

ISBN versión impresa en español 979-8-9865312-1-2

ISBN versión de libro electrónico en español 979-8-9865312-2-9

Edited by Jeanette Windle at www.jeanettewindle.com.

Cover designed by Endig Prayitno (J. Ferd) at www.99designs.com.

Book interior, final format, and ebook designed by Ebook Listing Services at www.ebooklistingservices.com.

Contact the author at billhilbradney@gmail.com.

Dedication

This book is dedicated to:

The One who planned and provided these stories enriching my life and countless others. My first thanks belong to Jesus!

My faithful, supportive husband of sixty years, our three children Ruth, Philip, and Cheryl, eight grandchildren, and four great-grandchildren.

Godly parents, teachers, colleagues, mentors, pastors, friends, and students who positively contributed to my personal story.

Lastly, I dedicate these stories to you, my reader, that you may discover secrets which will unlock doors to rewarding, purposeful living throughout your journey to eternity

Table of Contents

Dedication v

Introduction—Stories to Tell 1
Chapter 1—Accident, Flashlight and Papaya Leaves 3
Chapter 2— Pandemic to Purpose 8
Chapter 3—Tools to Treasures 13
Chapter 4—God's H&H Team 20
Chapter 5—Simla Adventure 25
Chapter 6— Down Under 30
Chapter 7—New Challenges 35
Chapter 8—Invitation to the USA 40
Chapter 9—Travelling, Tents, and Caravans 44
Chapter 10—Goodbye Australia 48
Chapter 11—Eastern Bible Institute 55
Chapter 12—Physical and Spiritual Giant 61
Chapter 13—The Hil-Billy Team 66
Chapter 14—A Solid Foundation 70
Chapter 15—Growing Church and Family 76
Chapter 16—Go and I Will Be With You! 83
Chapter 17— Loving and Learning Costa Rica 91
Chapter 18—Students Become Teachers 98
Chapter 19—Do Angels Wear Overalls? 105
Chapter 20—How Long Is Your Skirt? 111
Chapter 21—An Evil Day 118
Chapter 22— Reverse Culture Shock 125
Chapter 23—Leave within Ten Days! 130

Chapter 24—Humpty Dumpty ... 135
Chapter 25—Why Speak So Loudly? ... 140
Chapter 26—Dad Sent Us to Jail ... 145
Chapter 27—Escape from Death ... 151
Chapter 28—Ouch, My Band-Aid ... 157
Chapter 29—Five Dollars and a Heavenly Father ... 162
Chapter 30—More Student God-Encounters ... 167
Chapter 31—God's Divine Timing ... 172
Chapter 32—Beauty from Ugliness ... 176
Chapter 33— Adios Costa Rica ... 182
Chapter 34—Starting Again ... 187
Chapter 35—A Difficult Year ... 196
Chapter 36—Open Heart Surgery ... 201
Chapter 37—Running in High Heels ... 208
Chapter 38—Radical Contrasts, Different Perspectives ... 213
Chapter 39—Hora Feliz ... 220
Chapter 40—What's Heaven Like? ... 226
Chapter 41—A Walking Miracle ... 233
Chapter 42—Thieves! ... 237
Chapter 43—Another Adios ... 241
Chapter 44—Just the Way He Likes It! ... 246
Chapter 45—Divine Interventions in Costa Rica ... 250
Chapter 46—Dream Fulfilled ... 256
Chapter 47—More Divine Interventions ... 262
Chapter 48—Aussie Adventure ... 268
Epilogue—Not Retired But Retreaded ... 272

About the Author ... 277

"*My heart sings with thanks for my Lord . . .
for the Mighty One has done great things.*"
*—The Virgin Mary
Luke 1:46-49 NLV*

Introduction
Stories to Tell

We all have stories to tell. Stories that leave others laughing, crying, astonished, uplifted, and hopefully inspired. In my case, those stories begin with lessons of faith and courage I first learned from my godly parents, pioneer missionaries in India during some of history's most challenging seasons there, including on the front lines of World War II.

As the daughter of missionaries, then later serving with my husband as missionaries in Latin America, as well as through personal acquaintance with countries, cultures, and people across several continents, I have experienced firsthand and witnessed in other lives God's divine intervention, both natural and supernatural. He has interrupted, orchestrated, spoken, transformed, healed emotionally and physically, comforted, guided, protected, and provided with and without human involvement.

As I write this book, I realize that many involved in these stories or who have helped me collect them deserve a huge thank you. Seeing and hearing God work in the rich and poor, educated formally and informally, old and young around the world, I've discovered that the password to a happy heart is an attitude of thanks.

At the urging of many, I have dredged from my memory, documented, and researched the following stories I've experienced, witnessed, and heard. Countless others not recorded here are indelibly printed in heaven's books. It is my prayer that these stories will motivate reflection on how God has orchestrated your own life as well as to thank the Giver of "every good gift" (James 1:17 KJV) and those who have invested in you.

Chapter One

Accident, Flashlight, and Papaya Leaves

In October 1971, it had been a little over a year since my husband Bill and I with our three children had arrived in Costa Rica to serve as missionaries with the Assemblies of God. By now we were somewhat fluent in Spanish, and Bill had been invited to accompany a Costa Rican pastor to Cahuita, Costa Rica, a coastal village near the Panamanian border. The purpose of the trip was to encourage local Christians among the Bribri tribe, an indigenous people who lived in the jungle areas around Cahuita.

To get to Cahuita, the two men caught a night train. At 3.30 a.m., Bill and other passengers were settled into their seats trying to sleep when the train suddenly lurched, then braked to an abrupt, screeching standstill. Along with several other cars, the passenger car in which Bill and his travel companion were seated tore loose from the train, flipped over, and slid a good thirty to forty meters down a deep ravine. It finally came to rest against large rocks and underbrush.

With the passenger car upside-down, Bill struggled to orient himself on a ceiling that was now the floor. It didn't help that the kerosene lamps which were the passenger car's only lighting had been snuffed out, so he was in complete darkness. A quick check revealed that nothing seemed broken though Bill was bleeding from his nose and ears. Looking through a window, he spotted the light of the locomotive on the tracks high above.

Bill managed to locate his pastor friend. Along with the other passengers, they scrambled out of the overturned passenger car, grabbed onto bushes and tree trunks, and slowly crawled up the mountainside to where the remainder of the train still clung to the train tracks. Incredibly, no one looked seriously injured, though all were in shock and sporting bruises and cuts.

It was three hours before another train arrived to take injured passengers to a medical clinic. There was no electricity, so the medical assistant had to examine Bill with a flashlight. After a cursory examination, he informed my husband that he'd escaped any serious injury, then sent Bill on his way. Unfortunately, that wasn't the case. In the crash and scramble up the mountain, Bill had dislocated a disc in his back, though we didn't know at the time exactly what was wrong.

Over the following weeks and then months, Bill struggled with chronic back pain, exacerbated by bouts of malaria, hepatitis B, amebic dysentery, acute gastritis, and a bleeding ulcer. From a healthy 175 pounds for his height, he dwindled to 130 pounds. Many weeks, he slept on a blanket on the bedroom floor, where I fed him soft food by the teaspoon. He always tried to show a positive attitude, joking that if he stood up with his tongue out, he'd look like a zipper or that he'd need to stand up twice to make a shadow.

But I was growing increasingly desperate over Bill's deteriorating condition, especially with three small children to care for and ministry responsibilities as well. Where was God? If He had called us to serve Him in Costa Rica, why was He allowing all this to happen? One particularly challenging day, I cried out loudly to God, "Do you know where we live, Lord?"

While I was crying out to God, Bill was overcome with nausea. He began crawling painfully on his stomach along our bedroom floor into the tiled bathroom. Pushing himself up from the floor, he leaned over the toilet, vomiting. The retching and heaving placed even more strain on his hurting back.

Then suddenly one excruciating spasm led to a sudden *crack* along his spinal column. For the first time in months, he was able to straighten up without agonizing pain. Amazingly, the repeated jerking as he'd vomited had snapped the dislocated disc back into its proper location. Though he'd had to crawl into the bathroom, he was able to walk out on his feet, slowly but steadily.

As I rushed to my husband and discovered what had happened, my tears overflowed. My accusing prior demand changed to a prayer of thanksgiving and repentance. *Thank You, thank You, thank You for touching Bill! And I'm so, so sorry for my impatience, Jesus!*

I was left overwhelmed by God's presence and patience with me. This miraculous breakthrough was a reminder that Bill and I could face our future trusting in our loving heavenly Father. Though Bill would continue to battle occasional back pain until undergoing surgery on a trip to the United States, he was at least back on his feet and able to return to normal life and ministry

But Bill still struggled with some of his other health challenges. The Assemblies had a Bible Institute in San Jose, the capital of Costa Rica, that taught pastors and laymen God's Word and Christian discipleship. When the Bible Institute wasn't in session, faculty members would hold short-term Bible Institute sessions in various rural regions. For an entire week, local pastors and laymen would travel to a central locale, where they studied seven to eight hours daily, concluding each day with an open-air evangelistic outreach that included a gospel film.

Bill and another faculty member had taught one of these sessions in an indigenous Mayan village where the local tribal chief was among the Christian laymen attending the session. When the chief heard that Bill was sick with a serious case of hepatitis B, he took it upon himself to prepare an indigenous medical remedy, which involved painstakingly extracting the juice from tiny, new papaya leaves.

When the chief had a bottle full of the bright-green liquid, he sent his son on an eight-hour bus trip to bring the bottle to Bill. Today, papaya leaf extract is popular even in North America as a proven treatment for malaria, dengue fever, improving liver function, and other health benefits. But we were understandably wary at the time, so we checked with Vera, the Bible Institute cook, as to the extract's health benefits. She recommended its value.

Bill drank the extract. To his surprise, he was feeling much better by the very next day. He continued taking the extract and continued to improve. A later exam revealed that his liver, damaged by the hepatitis, was completely healed. We were so grateful to God and to this loving, caring Christian tribal chief.

This was just one example of how Costa Rican believers expressed their love to us in many practical ways over the years. It is also just one example of how God used what some might consider "natural" means to supernaturally intervene in our lives, whether keeping a hundred-foot plunge down an embankment from killing my husband, using a bout of nausea to adjust a dislocated spine, or giving wisdom to an indigenous tribal chief in applying nature's bounty to heal a tropical disease.

Chapter Two

Pandemic to Purpose

My own story begins with my parents' committed love of God and desire to serve Him, which abruptly and dramatically transformed their lives as two young, single adults in the aftermath of WW1 England. In 1925, my mother Hilda Newsham was twenty-four years old and enjoying a carefree life with a loving family, friends, and plenty of parties. During the week, she worked as a professional secretary at the Bank of London. On Sunday mornings, she attended the formal state church. Though she seemingly had everything she needed or wanted, Hilda's heart felt empty, and she wondered if there was something more to life.

Then Hilda's comfortable world suddenly crashed. Neither family, friends, medical specialists, nor her church could help. A medical specialist diagnosed Hilda's condition as the Spanish flu, a virus that between 1918-1921 alone infected an estimated one-third of the planet's population with a casualty count between fifty and a hundred million, making it one of the worst pandemics in human history. There was no medical treatment.

Hilda became increasingly weak and frail. Her dark hair, eyebrows, and eyelashes had fallen from her head. She was facing death when a bank coworker and friend invited Hilda to revival meetings at Surrey Tabernacle in Walworth, a district of South London, in June 1925. The evangelist speaking was Stephen Jeffreys, a former coal miner from South Wales, one of a hundred thousand recorded converts attributed to the preaching of famed Welsh evangelist Evan Roberts.

Hilda accepted the invitation. The revival was so popular that she had to wait in line for hours to get into the tabernacle. Finding a front-row balcony seat, she listened with astonishment as a packed auditorium of all ages worshipfully sang from colored song sheets. What a stark contrast from the Church of England's strict liturgy! How could a preacher not even properly robed speak with such authority from a religious platform?

But Jeffrey's compassion and sincerity captured Hilda's heart. It seemed he was speaking directly to her, then describing her life to the thousands packed in the building. Deeply impacted, Hilda returned night after night. One evening, she joined the human stream down to the altar to ask Christ's forgiveness for her sins.

As Stephen Jeffrey prayed over those who had come to the altar, Hilda felt God's power flow like electricity through her body. At that moment, she was not only forgiven of sin but instantly healed and Spirit-filled. As she knelt there at the altar, she received a divine vision of dark faces crowded around carved wooden arched doors. Recognizing the faces as being of East India ethnicity, Hilda concluded that God was directing her to serve Him in India.

Bubbling over with joy, she excitedly shared with her family how God had transformed her. Her shocked parents and brothers couldn't deny there had been a transformation. The weak, frail

Hilda who had been close to death was now happy and strong. Just three days saw a growth of hair and in two weeks little black curls. Her doctor confirmed her recovery but had no medical explanation.

This miracle brought the entire family to vibrant faith in God. Hilda thrived spiritually as she began studying God's Word and attending any gospel service she could. She soon discovered that Stephen Jeffreys was associated with the Elim Evangelistic Band, later known as the Elim Pentecostal Church. The name Elim signifies oasis, referring to the biblical account of the Israelites as they wandered through the desert (Exodus 15:27).

Making an appointment with Elim's director of missions, Hilda blurted out excitedly, "God has called me to India!"

The response was anything but positive. The missions director told her bluntly, "We aren't appointing single missionaries since we have a long list of couples and families waiting to serve in needy countries around the world."

Convinced God had called her to serve in India, Hilda was not deterred. Though she did no formal fundraising, family members and friends gave her enough checks to cover her boat passage to India. Fare in hand, she returned to the Elim mission director. The Elim evangelistic organization then gladly blessed her as one of their missionaries. As my mother prepared to travel to India, another missionary wrote the following poem for her farewell commissioning service.

No rose-petalled pathway to walk on,
No velvety, grass-covered way,
But stones and a desert and an outpost
And a cross to carry always.
There's sin to be dealt with and sinning.
There's a fight to be fought just by you.
But there's glory ahead for the follower
And a victory that's always true.
So pick up your armor and wear it,
Grip firmly the Sword in your hand,
And the power that has called you to battle
Will see that you also can stand.

It was 1933 when Hilda arrived with her meager luggage at India's northeast port of Calcutta, known today as Kolkata. Looking down from the boat's deck at her new home, the land of her calling, Hilda immediately noticed the tall, ornate doors of the customs building that was the entry point for every new arrival. The doors were carved, wooden, and arched just as she'd seen in her vision that memorable night in Surrey Tabernacle. God, who had healed her and called her to India, was now empowering her to enter these ornate doors to serve Him.

Hilda attended language school to learn Hindi, India's most predominant language, then began ministering and teaching God's Word in the Calcutta area with another Elim missionary, Miss Ewens. This was not an easy assignment since Calcutta was then and still is one of the world's most congested, dirty, disease-filled, smelly cities. Hilda's first major spiritual challenge came from a desperate Indian mother.

"Lady, I have heard that your God is greater than Satan. If that's true, will you please cast Satan out from my son?"

As Hilda prayed over the woman's son in Jesus's name, the boy was delivered from Satan's control. Mother and son became part of a growing new group of believers that were Hilda's responsibility to disciple in Bible truths. Reading Christ's command for water baptism, many asked to be baptized. Hilda was only four feet, eight inches tall, so baptizing those taller than her was a challenge. She creatively brought in a bathtub. Baptismal candidates knelt in the water, enabling her to easily baptize them.

Historical records from Elim Pentecostal Church, now a denomination with more than four thousand Pentecostal churches in over fifty countries globally, show that that on January 15, 1934, Hilda Newsham celebrated the opening of House of Prayer, the first Pentecostal church building erected in Calcutta. During the ceremony, an earthquake shook the city for eight minutes. The congregation rushed out of the sanctuary into the surrounding compound. The building swayed and windows rattled, but there was no loss of life. During special meetings over the following two weeks, God healed bodies and saved souls, and many received the Holy Spirit's infilling.

I am forever grateful for my mother, who obeyed God's sacred call faithfully and lovingly, serving her Lord and Savior until her final breath when angels escorted her to her heavenly home.

Chapter Three

Tools to Treasure

My father Harold Groves was born in Portsmouth, England, in 1908. His father Albert Groves, a petty officer in the Royal Navy for twenty-two years, was drowned in 1916 when his ship was torpedoed during a World War 1 battle with the German fleet. This left his mother with eight-year-old Harold as well as a younger brother and sister. As the oldest, Harold begged his mother to let him quit school so he could help provide for the family.

Harold began working for his mother's brother delivering furniture on a cart. This was very hard labor for a young boy. One day while struggling to push an especially heavy cart over a bridge, he breathed a prayer: *God, please help me!* Just then, an old man passing by stopped to help Harold push the cart. This made clear to Harold that God had heard his prayer.

During this time, Harold's uncle was sexually abusing him. Harold knew how much his mother loved her brother, so he didn't feel he could tell her. In desperation, he looked up to heaven and cried out, "God, I have no earthly father. If You are up there, will You please help me?"

The next morning when Harold entered the furniture store to begin work, he saw his uncle in suit and tie lying motionless on the floor. He immediately called the police, who pronounced his uncle dead. Once again, Harold recognized that God had answered his prayer in His own mysterious way.

To help support the family, Harold decided to start his own business. Looking in the local Woolworth store's window, he saw some attractive metal tea trays on sale. With the British penchant for tea and pastries, he figured tea trays could be a profitable sales item. He had enough money left from prior earnings to buy twelve tea trays. Then he began knocking on house doors. Sometimes owners slammed their doors, but Harold persisted. Soon he had sold all the trays.

Returning to Woolworths, he bought two more dozen trays. Selling those, he bought some more. Eventually, he was purchasing a hundred trays at a time, selling them to both individuals and tea shops. He was proud to be such a good salesman and help his family. At the same time, he was embarrassed to be a school dropout.

On one occasion while he was peddling trays, Harold saw a former schoolmate crossing to his side of the road. He immediately stooped down and pretended to tie his shoelace so his former schoolmate wouldn't see him working as a common hawker. Only after his classmate went by without spotting him did Harold stand up and begin hawking his trays again.

Later, Harold began buying, repairing, polishing, and selling used motorcycles. One day, he bought a used sports car, its outside exhaust attached with rope, for only twelve pounds. Acquiring the necessary driver's license, Harold began driving it around. Falling in love with the car, a neighbor asked Harold, "How much do you want for it?"

"Forty pounds," Harold quickly responded.

"Done deal!" the neighbor replied.

It was Harold's first big turn of profit. But the first day the neighbor drove it, he accelerated and smashed into his garden wall. His wife ran out with a rolling pin in hand, yelling at him to get rid of the car. The unhappy neighbor quickly found a buyer and sold the sports car for just ten pounds.

As Harold's savings grew, he bought tools at good sales prices, storing them under his bed. When he had enough money, he paid one month's rent on a neighborhood store and proudly displayed his tools in the store window. Talented in signwriting, he made a sign that read: *Groves Hardware Open for Business.* At fifteen years of age, he was now a businessowner.

Business flourished. Harold opened two more stores. He also imported one of the first key-cutting machines from the United States and added that to his business ventures. Harold's keen aptitude for business would serve him well throughout his life. God was preparing him to promote and share the gospel message to individuals and large crowds around the world.

One day a friend named Stephen Laws invited Harold to go with him to hear Welsh evangelist George Jeffries, brother of Stephen Jeffries. Harold didn't want to offend his friend, who was also a very good customer, so he suggested, "Stephen, I will attend with you if you'll ride there with me on my Triumph motorbike."

Harold figured he was off the hook since Stephen knew Harold loved to speed and had been denied insurance because of his poor driving record. To Harold's surprise, his friend agreed to the ride. Stephen later admitted, "I hung on tightly, praying all the way!"

Once at the revival meeting, Harold wanted to sit in the back for an easy escape, but Stephen led Harold to the front row. As evangelist George Jeffreys explained God's wonderful plan of salvation, Harold noticed a woman seated nearby in a wheelchair. Once the evangelist finished preaching and prayed, the woman stood up straight and asked her husband to sit in the chair so she could push him. After witnessing this miracle, Harold asked Jesus to save him from his sin and committed his life to following his Saviour. He kept his unconditional commitment to love and serve God until he died.

This experience sparked a hunger in Harold for more of God. Harold's business neighbor, a tailor who had also recently accepted Christ, invited Harold to join him in prayer on Wednesdays when the local stores closed at noon. Kneeling together each Wednesday afternoon, the two businessmen prayed. Sometimes Stephen joined them. One afternoon, Harold began praising God in a language he hadn't learned. Stephen excitedly told Harold he'd received what early followers of Jesus received at Pentecost (Acts 2).

"What was that?" asked Harold.

"The Holy Spirit is empowering you to be God's witness," Stephen responded.

Harold soon joined a Pentecostal church. One day Harold took a non-believing uncle to hear Pentecostal evangelist Smith Wigglesworth. A woman seated nearby had a nasty uncovered sore on her hand. Harold was uncomfortable to see it as he knew his uncle would be critical of the woman's plight. While the entire audience prayed aloud, Harold's uncle kept staring at this large sore. By the time the prayer time concluded, the ugly sore had disappeared and the woman's hand showed only clean flesh. After witnessing this miracle, Harold's uncle asked Jesus into his life. He and Harold took the step of being baptized in water at the same time.

Harold had heard visiting missionaries speak of India's great need. He felt in his heart that God wanted him to serve in India. His pastor also affirmed that God's hand was on Harold for fulltime service. To prepare himself for ministry, Harold entered Hampstead Bible School, an Assemblies of God college in South London. The director Howard Carter instilled in the students a love of God's Word and emphasized that faith pleases God, encouraging students to believe God for His miraculous interventions.

In 1930 while Harold was attending Hampstead, Howard Carter shared with the students a need to expand the college's limited facilities. The director had made a down-payment on a larger building. When the closing date approached, the college still didn't have money to pay the balance. Carter asked the students to pray.

"If we don't have the finances by tomorrow, we will lose a very substantial deposit," he explained.

That evening as the student body and faculty gathered to pray for the necessary funds to come in, a visiting missionary from France, Pastor Douglas Scott, prophesied that buckets full of money would come in. The students puzzled over this strange prophecy. After praying until midnight, they were heading to bed when they heard a loud thump at the front door.

Harold was first to rush down stairs. Opening the door, he spotted a number of newspaper-wrapped bundles. When he opened one, he found cash inside. He called the other students to come down. There was so much money they had to fetch buckets to carry it all in. That's when the students remembered the visiting missionary's bucket prophecy. When the money was counted, it was enough to cover the entire purchase of the new property. God had poured out His Spirit in that school!

After his studies at Hampstead, Harold married a young woman named Iris who was also a committed Christian and in agreement with God's call to missions in India. Together they visited nineteenth-century evangelist George Mueller's orphanage in Bristol, England. Starting in his rented home, Mueller had eventually cared for thousands of children in orphanages. Rather than ask for contributions, he'd taken the children's needs directly to his heavenly Father. Daily, the administration and children had witnessed miracles of God's provision.

Greatly inspired by Mueller's example, Harold and Iris decided that if God could miraculously provide for thousands of precious children, then He could take care of them as they followed God's direction to India. Approaching the Assemblies of God mission board, they informed the board that they'd like to go to India without raising any financial support.

Selling his three stores, Harold purchased tickets. The young couple sailed to India in September 1932. But within six months of arriving in India, Iris succumbed to malaria and died. Refusing to allow his tragic loss to derail the mission to which God had called him, Harold joined an older Assemblies of God missionary couple ministering in a small Indian town.

I'm so grateful for Dad, who trusted God, refusing to give up.

Chapter Four
God's H&H Team

In God's wisdom and timing, my mother Hilda invited an evangelist for revival meetings in the newly formed House of Prayer. Unable to come, the evangelist sent another missionary in his stead, a young, handsome English widower. Harold Groves's sincere love for God, dynamic preaching, and violin playing captured Hilda's heart.

In the Indian culture, courtship was unacceptable since marriages were arranged by the parents. Though Hilda wasn't aware of it at the time, the House of Prayer congregation, concerned about her unmarried state, had decided to stand in for her parents since they were in England and had actually chosen a nice Indian Christian man as her bridegroom. But the arrival of an eligible Christian widower of her own nationality changed their plans. Harold and Hilda married within weeks of meeting in early 1934.

The newly-weds decided to withdraw from both their mission agencies and trust God for direction and provision. Over the next several decades until God called my mother into His divine presence, Harold and Hilda faithfully loved and served God together, bringing countless people to faith and discipling them to be true witnesses of Jesus Christ.

Harold and Hilda rented a small house in Calcutta as their own residence. With what little funds they had, my father decided to emulate the apostle Paul's trade as tentmaker and create a large tent to hold evangelistic services, a first at that time in Calcutta. Harold purchased rolls of canvas, rented twelve foot-treadle sewing machines, and hired twelve men to sew. The ensuing tent was a hundred feet long by fifty feet wide.

The tent held about five hundred people. Harold and Hilda set up chairs and placed a small box by the entrance for those wanting to give an offering. About four hundred people came to the first service. Souls were saved, God miraculously healed many, and there was great joy. The little box by the door was crammed with money. God had supplied Harold and Hilda's financial needs and did so ever since. That was the birth of my parents' ministry as a couple.

Among those who came to Christ in those tent meetings was Indian businessman G.E. Silas. At the time, he had a small, rented store that sold toothpaste and a few medicines. As Harold discipled him in God's Word, Silas began to tithe and soon became a prosperous businessman. He eventually became the president of India's branch of the Gideon Bible Society, which has placed Bibles in hotel rooms and in the hands of people of every walk of life across the globe since 1908.

Years later while visiting the United States, Harold received a call from the international president of GBS, asking, "Are you Mr. Groves who worked in India in 1932?"

"Yes," Harold replied.

"I congratulate you," the President continued. "A man named G.E. Silas who found Christ in one of your tent revival meetings in Calcutta is with me now as the invited speaker for our annual convention. Silas has raised millions of dollars, breaking all previous records, to distribute Gideon Bibles worldwide."

The arrival of the monsoon rains made it difficult to hold services in a tent. Howard and Hilda rented a church building, where they ministered for several years until a beautiful church was given to them free of cost by the London Missionary Society.

During this time period, Aimee Semple McPherson, well-known Pentecostal evangelist and pastor of Angelus Temple in Los Angeles, California, one of the earliest megachurches, came to Calcutta. My parents hosted meetings with her. Founder of the Foursquare fellowship of churches, Aimee was also acclaimed as a pioneer in using the new technology of radio to broadcast her church services to millions.

By this time, Harold and Hilda were already proud parents of two girls, Joy and Pauline. Joy was four-and-a-half-years old and Pauline just three when another daughter was added to the Groves family in August 1939. At that time, prejudice against women was engrained into Indian culture, and the doctor who delivered me refused to advise Dad that Mother had borne him another girl.

But Dad loved his three daughters, referring to them privately and publicly as his "three bonnie girls." This was a testimony and blessing to Indian families that only had daughters in a context where boys were far more desired and valued. My parents named me after my mother. Hilda means warrior maid, and I have prayed throughout my life that I would characterize a true servant of God fighting "the good fight of faith" (1 Timothy 6:12 KJV).

Chapter Four: God's H&H Team

During World War II, aggressive attacks by the Japanese led to great desperation among both the local Indian population and Allied troops stationed in Calcutta. At that time, India was a major aerial supply route to China for the Allied forces. Since Burma, now Myanmar, had been occupied by the Japanese, supply planes had to cross the Himalayan mountains along a dangerous route called the Hump to airlift supplies to Allied war efforts in China.

Curfews, rationing, restrictions, and fear gripped Calcutta's dense population. Starving refugees poured in, many of whom died before finding food. My older sister Pauline, six years old at this time, remembers trucks hauling away decomposing corpses. Mother bravely rode her bicycle to pray for the sick and needy.

Food was scarce for all of us, and we counted it a special treat when American and English soldiers shared tins of Nestles Condensed Milk and other items from their rations with our family. My sisters and I were also delighted when they gave us piggyback rides and shared sweets with us.

In the midst of such violence and despair, revival meetings held by my parents drew both British and American soldiers as well as Indians in morning and nightly services. Many were led to Jesus and miraculously healed while those possessed and oppressed by Satanic forces were freed to love and serve God. After conversion, soldiers often requested water baptism before they returned to battle frontlines. Because water was rationed, the baptistry was left undrained between baptisms. One soldier celebrated God's transformation by shouting: "To Jesus! Hip-hip-hurray! Hip-hip-hurray! Hip-hip-hurray!"

The Groves Family in India.

Chapter Five

Simla Adventure

Though he was pastoring a growing congregation in Calcutta, Dad had a strong call from God's Spirit that he was to plant a church in Simla, a beautiful town in the Himalayan foothills more than a thousand miles from Calcutta that was known as the British India summer capital. Missionary friends about to transition to another area of service offered to pastor the Calcutta congregation for six months so our family could go to Simla.

It was the height of World War II when our family left by train for Simla in January 1942. After a tiring three-day trip, we arrived at Simla's railway station. The train's open windows had left a residue of sand and soot on our clothing, so Mother tidied us girls while Dad walked about a mile into Simla's main shopping area. As far as he knew, Dad had no acquaintances in Simla, but as he was walking, he suddenly heard a man shout from the other side of the street, "Praise the Lord, Brother Groves!"

The man and his wife were Lithuanian missionary doctors who had visited the Groves's church in Calcutta. At that very moment, a woman who lived on the street where Dad was walking opened her front door. An immigrant from Ireland, Miss Sullivan was a devout Christian, and her attention was immediately caught by the doctor's "Praise the Lord!"

Approaching, Miss Sullivan began asking questions. "What is your name? Do you have a family? Are you interested in accommodation?"

"Harold Groves," Dad responded. "And yes, actually, my family is at the railway station right now. We've come to Simla to see what God has planned."

"Well, I have three guesthouses I rent out during the summer hot season," Miss Sullivan went on. "Just an hour ago, I received a telegram cancelling accommodation for a brigadier general right here in this very guesthouse. His accommodation was already pre-paid for six months, so you're welcome to stay here. In fact, you're just in time for lunch."

Amazed at God's miraculous provision, Dad hurried back to us at the railway station and announced excitedly, "Come with me! Just a mile from here, a lady has lunch waiting for us in a lovely guesthouse."

A neighbor next-door to the guesthouse owned a three-story building. The top floor housed a restaurant, the second a movie theater, while the ground floor held a skating rink. Renting the ground floor for a one-month campaign, Dad printed advertising leaflets to distribute and started nightly revival meetings.

Over the next months, God moved in a powerful way. Many accepted Christ and were filled with God's Spirit. One child had a vision of heaven. She described crystal-clear water emanating from

God's throne (Revelation 22:1). She also saw her brother Johnny. Only after the service did she discover that Johnny had died an hour before her vision. A Baptist pastor's children publicly accepted Jesus as their Savior. Their father invited Dad to baptize the new believers in his nearby church.

Miss Sullivan had witnessed revival in Ireland. Now she was witnessing God move in her current hometown of Simla, India. At seventy years old, she had no relatives, so she decided to make her will in Dad's favor. Dad refused, concerned that this might prove a temptation to keep him from obeying God's will to evangelize in India.

During this time, my older sister Pauline was diagnosed with meningitis, double pneumonia, and typhoid fever. Weakened and unable to walk, she lay in bed for months. Mother was threatened with legal action for refusing to admit Pauline to a local hospital, but she knew her care was superior to the local medical system. Satanic rituals and worship were prevalent in Simla, and my parents fought a constant spiritual battle. Mother wrote out and prayed specific scriptures that she attached to Pauline's bedroom walls.

Decades later when Pauline and I visited our aging father in Bangalore, India, I was invited to share God's Word in a Sunday morning evangelical church service. At the conclusion, the pastor expressed his delight to see us. He was especially excited to see an adult Pauline healthy and strong. He explained that he'd been among new believers Dad had led to Christ in his hometown of Simla when Dad invited them to join the family in prayer for Pauline.

"We climbed the stairs and circled Pauline's bed," the pastor continued. "All of us in the room sensed an evil presence. Together we submitted ourselves to God and resisted Satan as taught in in James 4:7. Immediately, we saw a black form leave the room and the property."

While as a three-year-old I have no memory of that event, God did indeed touch Pauline's weak body. After that prayer session, she immediately got out of bed and was soon back to normal, enjoying life. This miracle very much strengthened these new followers of Jesus in Simla.

While in Simla, my parents took a multi-day hike along a popular Himalayan hiking trail where government rest houses along the way offered room and board. Towards the end of their second day on the trail, they heard gospel singing from a residence. Dad knocked on the door. A woman answered the door. Beyond her was the group of people who had been singing.

My parents introduced themselves. Inviting them inside, the woman explained that she was a Christian doctor, then went on, "We were holding a house church meeting when you heard us singing. We love Jesus. But we'd like more."

My parents shared God's promise and outpouring of the Holy Spirit in Acts 1-2, and all present received the gift of God's Holy Spirit. My parents stayed there for the night, then continued their hike the following day.

Though Dad had rejected Miss Sullivan's offer to bequeath him her Simla properties, he discovered after she passed away that she'd made Dad her sole beneficiary. Sadly, a man named Dutt employed a corrupt lawyer to forge Dad's signature, misappropriating the entire estate. Dad left the injustice in God's hands.

Sometime after the misappropriation, a Christian customs official, Brother Chandra, invited both Dad and Mr. Dutt to his home. Mr. Dutt was already seated when Dad was ushered in. Astonished to see the man he'd defrauded, Mr. Dutt turned bright-red, crumpled off his chair, and died. As with Dad's abusive uncle, God had answered prayer and delivered justice in His own mysterious way.

For six months, my parents discipled new believers. By the time we returned to Calcutta, a strong church had been planted in Simla just as Dad had felt called to do. But Calcutta and all of India was soon to be only a faint memory for me.

Chapter Six
Down Under

In December 1942, Calcutta was jolted awake by bomb blasts as the Japanese air force began bombing the city. While the Allied fighter pilots destroyed many Japanese bombers, saving much of Calcutta's infrastructure, Japanese air raids continued sporadically throughout 1943 and into 1944, when Japan redeployed its air force elsewhere.

An early memory as a three-year-old is accompanying my parents and sisters to visit Chinese neighbors who lived in a house with fortified walls. From their flat roof, we watched the bombing all around Calcutta for a few minutes, then prudently retreated downstairs.

Toward the end of 1943, a small Pentecostal church in Adelaide, a seaport in southern Australia, heard about the Groves family living with their young daughters in a dangerous war zone in Calcutta. The church elders offered to pay expenses so our family could leave India for a year and pastor their congregation. Dad went first by boat to investigate the offer. After assuring himself this was where God wanted our family, he telegraphed Mother to come with the three girls.

Chapter Six: Down Under

Mother found a cargo ship traveling to Australia and booked our passage. She was the only woman onboard while my two sisters and I were the only children. Many ships in those dangerous seas were torpedoed by the Japanese, but God protected us, and we arrived safely in Adelaide to a warm welcome. Dad rented the Adelaide town hall for nightly services, where many families came to Christ, were baptized in water, and received the gift of the Holy Spirit.

Our family of five moved into the church parsonage. Mother enrolled my two sisters and me in Methodist Ladies' College, a private elementary school, to which we travelled by tramcar. Though still only four, I was in kindergarten. The school uniform included wine-colored jumpers, white shirts, ties, hats, and oxford shoes. Manners and conduct were high priority, and infractions inside and outside campus were reported. Uniforms and shoes were inspected daily.

Sundays were especially busy, starting with morning worship, a bagged lunch eaten in the church fellowship hall, afternoon Sunday School, followed by tea. We then walked downtown to a street meeting where we sang gospel songs accompanied by a portable pump organ and believers testified to God's transforming power. Passersby stopped to listen, and many accepted an invitation to the evening service.

Dad also bought Mother a small motorcycle for her personal transport during the week. When we weren't in school, my sisters and I would take turns accompanying her on the back of the motorcycle to visit and pray for those in need.

At the conclusion of a year pastoring the Adelaide congregation, Dad felt he needed to return to the group of believers in Calcutta. He wanted Mother to accompany him, but the extended war made it too dangerous to take small children.

Two of the church families offered to care for us for the six months my parents initially planned to be gone. My younger sister Pauline and I stayed with a delightful church couple, Harold and Rita Bradshaw, who had always longed for children but couldn't conceive. They treated us as though we were their own children, providing us a stable, loving environment and teaching us how to love God, life, and others.

Pauline and I were extremely happy with the Bradshaws. One special memory was a three-week holiday at the quaint coastal town of Port Elliot where Uncle Harold took us rock scrambling, fishing, building sandcastles, and jumping waves. Sadly, we had no idea until many years later that my older sister Joy, who lived with another church family, was very unhappy and suffered greatly the absence of our parents.

Auntie Rita taught Pauline and me to knit, so while travelling by tram car, we knitted our own sweaters and other items. Still just five years old, I was unable to hang on to the tram's high leather straps or reach a seat handle, so I hung on to Pauline's braids, which formed a loop tied by a ribbon. When the tram jerked to stop, we both piled into other squeezed-in passengers. We later transferred to a public school to which we were able to walk.

Chapter Six: Down Under

According to Auntie Rita and Uncle Harold, Pauline and I were usually well-behaved. But one day when we returned from school, we didn't find Auntie Rita at home. Shedding our uniforms for play clothes, we ran across the street to play in a neighbor child's treehouse. Soon we heard Auntie Rita's voice urgently calling our names. We knew we weren't supposed to leave the house without permission, so we didn't move or answer.

Auntie Rita looked frantically from house to house, As her urgent calls grew more distant, we quickly climbed down the tree and dashed home. Ashamed and scared that we'd disobeyed the rules, we decided to hide in the dog's kennel, which was between the garage and neighbor's fence.

Frustrated and worried, Auntie Rita finally called Uncle Harold at work. Pauline and I were still squeezed into the kennel, cramped and suffocating, when he arrived. When we heard them debating whether they should call the police, we knew we were in serious trouble. Then to our despair, the dog joined the search. Tracing us to his kennel, he barked loudly.

In tears, we crawled out and ran into Auntie Rita and Uncle Harold's arms. In his firm but loving way, Uncle Harold sat us both on his lap and related the story of Adam and Eve's sin in the Garden of Eden and how they'd hidden in shame after sinning.

"But God found them," he added. "And He forgives us when we repent."

As Uncle Harold led us in prayer, Pauline and I both asked and received forgiveness. How relieved we were, forgiven and secure in his embrace. Pauline and I are forever grateful to the Bradshaws for accepting and loving us.

But while Auntie Rita and Uncle Harold provided love and security, we greatly missed our parents, especially our dear mother. One day Auntie Rita sunned Mother's winter clothing, which had been packed away in a metal trunk, on the outside clothesline. Wrapping myself in Mother's coat, I begged Auntie Rita not to repack Mother's clothing.

My parents' anticipated six-month absence ended up extending to over two years. Letters from them arrived by boat mail only sporadically after several months. My sisters and I kept these precious air-letter communications under our pillows to read and reread.

By now, WW2 had ended. Mother had some health issues, so she traveled from India to England for medical treatment, then continued on to Australia, where she was reunited with her three daughters. Dad followed several months later. At last our entire family was together again.

Chapter Seven
New Challenges

Dad accepted an invitation to pastor a church in Newcastle, New South Wales, another Australian port city on the opposite coast from Adelaide near the city of Sydney. I was now eight years old. The five of us lived in rooms behind the church building. One of its outreaches was to help recently arrived immigrants from Poland, Ukraine, and Russia. My parents opened their hearts and the church building for Sunday afternoon services to these refugees, many of whom had escaped severe persecution in their Communist homelands because of their unwavering faith in Jesus Christ.

The transition from Adelaide to Newcastle was a difficult one for my sisters and myself as we tried to fit into new schools and make new friends. To lift our spirits, Mother would take us to the nearby beach. The sand was blackened by coal dust, but Mother insisted the salty sea air would blow away the cobwebs in our brains.

As another treat, she took us to the wharf, where we fished with simple fishing-lines. The fish we caught were small fish and impossible to bone. Sailors on the docked ships offered us coins if we could catch a certain number of these tiny fish. We minced the fish in a meat grinder to make delicious fish patties.

One day a church member invited us girls to their farm. We were surprised to meet their twelve sons, the last one named Benjamin just like Jacob's twelfth son in the Old Testament (Genesis 35). They gave us a darling tiny puppy as well as fresh eggs.

Returning home on the bus, my sisters and I each sat in different available seats. Animals weren't allowed on the bus, so my oldest sister Joy kept the whimpering puppy tucked away in her dress pocket. I gingerly balanced the eggs in a brown paper bag on my lap while knitting with white angora wool. Pauline checked directions. When it was time to get off, she pulled the cord to advise the driver.

I quickly wrapped up my knitting project. But as I did so, some of the eggs I was carrying broke, making a mess on my dress, the seat, and the lady sitting next to me. Joy and Pauline had already exited the bus, but I lingered to clean up the sticky mess. I was horrified when the bus started up again. Just eight years old, I was now alone on a bus with strangers.

On tiptoes, I reached for the cord. At the next stop, I dismounted with dirty clothes, broken eggs, and stained knitting. It was now dark. Terrified, I dodged drunken men as I hurried back down the street to where my sisters were looking around for me, wondering where I was and why I hadn't followed them off the bus.

We huddled close together for moral support until we reached home. I ran into the house. As soon as I saw Mother, I burst into tears, releasing my pent-up emotions. Mother's hug and fragrance from her favorite *Eau-de-Cologne 4711* assured me I was safe and secure.

Chapter Seven: New Challenges

The seaport city of Newcastle was known for its extensive coalfields. A church member who directed one of the largest mines invited our church youth for a tour. Though too young for the youth group, I was allowed to tag along with my mother and sisters. We descended into the earth's black cavern in an open-iron coal cart on rails, where we watched the miners with lighted helmets expertly and carefully excavate. The boss invited Mother to discharge dynamite to release veins of coal. The process was most interesting, informative, and loudly ear-piercing.

We had been in Newcastle about two years when Dad decided it was time to move to Melbourne, the coastal capital of Australia's most southern state of Victoria. Though we didn't live there long, this move became a turning point in my life. I had now turned eleven years old and was well aware that I was a sinner. In fact, my sin was a constant heavy weight on me.

Most notably, I knew I'd become a thief. This had started back at the Bradshaws in Adelaide. Aunty Rita kept delicious frog-shaped chocolates in a large glass jar. Since she never kept count, I often took chocolate frogs to school. I knew this was wrong since we weren't supposed to help ourselves without permission.

Later when we were living in Newcastle, Mother occasionally sent me to buy groceries at the neighborhood store. While the grocer weighed out sugar or flour, I quietly reached over the counter to take displayed candy. I also stole coins to buy sweets at school by shaking Pauline's piggy bank where she kept her pocket money.

Now in our new home in Melbourne, I would do anything rather than go to bed because I knew I wasn't ready to meet Jesus. We had three single beds in our bedroom for the three sisters. I pushed my bed next to Pauline's and lifted her bed coverings so I could hang on to her. I knew she loved Jesus, so my thought was that if Jesus came in the night, I would go up to heaven with her. But I quickly realized that once we were asleep, Pauline and I would both unconsciously move or turn over. This meant I could lose my grip on Pauline, a predicament that added to my dreaded nightly dilemma.

One late night I couldn't stand the Holy Spirit's conviction any longer. With a heavy heart, I crept into my parents' bedroom. In tears, I blurted out, "I need to tell you something important. I'm a thief and want to get right with the Lord."

"Hilda, the Lord is waiting for you," Mother responded.

I confessed my sins and asked God to forgive me. Then my parents and I thanked God together. The weight of guilt rolled off my heart, and I felt free as a bird.

I still thank Jesus continuously for that beginning of a far-from-perfect but grace-filled, guilt-free life!

The Groves Family in Australia.

Chapter Eight
Invitation to the USA

Not long after our move to Melbourne, Dad read reports in *Voice of Healing* magazines of how God was uniquely using an American couple named T.L. and Daisy Osborn as evangelists in the United States and internationally. The articles mentioned they were from Oklahoma, so he wondered if they could possibly be the young couple my parents had encouraged while they were serving in Calcutta.

T. L. and Daisy Osborn were married in 1942 at eighteen and seventeen years old respectively. After a two year stint as itinerant pastors and evangelists, they felt called to serve as missionaries in India. They arrived in India at the end of WW2 but stayed less than a year. When my parents met them, they were still just twenty-one and twenty-two years old and had recently gone through the loss of their first baby boy. They'd seen no fruit from their evangelistic efforts. Discouraged and grieving, they'd decided to return to their home country and never leave it again.

The Osborns were in Calcutta awaiting passage on a troop ship back to the United States when my parents went to visit them in the small, rundown hotel where they were staying. This God-planned meeting changed the young couple's hearts and future. For several weeks as they awaited their ship, the Osborns listened to Dad preach and teach at the Calcutta church and witnessed God transforming broken lives and families.

As T.L. stated later, the power, wisdom, and thoroughness of Dad's teaching had a profound and revolutionary effect on his own spirit. The Osborns were also greatly impressed that this British missionary couple didn't accept missionary salaries but lived entirely on faith for God's provision. This had a great influence on their own future ministry.

After T.L. and Daisy returned to the United States, God continued to work powerfully in them, and in time they became among the best-known Pentecostal evangelists in North America and around the world. Decades later, T.L. Osborn wrote me a letter concerning my parents. Among other expressions of gratitude, he stated:

> *Harold Groves was the man that God used to change my life. Because we were popular young evangelists at home, our organization sent us to India as missionaries totally unprepared and incapable of dealing with the ancient religions of India. Our musical instruments were crushed in route. We miserably failed . It was your precious father teaching in Calcutta who first opened my spirit to the wonder of the Old and New Testaments coalescing and how Jesus*

was the entire subject of sacred Scriptures. Your precious papa prepared my spirit for God's visitations and the guidance of the Holy Spirit in our lives to share Christ with the world . Harold Groves showed me Jesus in every detail . In addition, [Harold and Hilda] Groves loved us, took interest in us, helped us, and I could say they healed us.

I am so grateful Mother and Dad allowed God to use them in changing the life trajectory of a very young, discouraged missionary couple. They could never have imagined then the major role T.L. and Daisy Osborn would eventually play in our own family's lives.

By 1950, just five years after my parents had met the Osborns in Calcutta, T. L. and Daisy had become well-known evangelists affiliated with the Voice of Healing association. The young couple who never wanted to leave their home country again were not only holding revival meetings and crusades all across the United States but traveling to other countries like Jamaica and Cuba. Not only were countless people coming to Christ, but they were seeing many healings and miracles. In fact, over the next two decades, the Osborns would preach to millions in over forty nations, and their global ministry continued until they stepped into glory after more than sixty years each of ministry.

But at that point in 1950, the Osborns realized they needed help with the crowds filling stadiums and open-air arenas nightly to hear from God. Remembering the blessing Harold and Hilda Groves had been to them in their season of grief and discouragement in Calcutta, they researched and found our Australian address. Letters crisscrossed the ocean.

In late 1950, just a few months after we moved to Melbourne, my parents asked Pauline and me if we'd like to return for a while to Auntie Rita and Uncle Harold Bradshaw. We were delighted at the prospect. Now fifteen, Joy had become a gifted musician, so my parents decided she would travel with them to help with playing the piano and organ. For the next year and a half, Mother, Dad, and Joy joined the Osborn team ministering throughout the United States.

Pauline and I were happy to be staying again with the Bradshaws in Adelaide. We both attended a neighborhood public school. Looking back, I am again so thankful to Auntie Rita and Uncle Harold for their love and support during our formation years.

Chapter Nine

Travelling, Tents, and Caravans

When Dad, Mother, and Joy returned to Australia in 1952, Dad felt God calling him to plant churches and boost local congregations across Australia. He ordered a large meeting tent, five hundred metal folding chairs, an imported electronic Hammond organ, a table for book sales, a truck in which to haul equipment, and a sixteen-foot caravan, or camper trailer in American, in which our family of five lived.

My bed was a space smaller than my body in between the icebox and Pauline's lower bunkbed. Joy slept in the top bunk. When we travelled, Dad drove the truck, which pulled the caravan, while Mother drove an open-backed station wagon in which we girls travelled. All of us worked together to unload chairs and equipment and erect the tent.

During services, Joy played the organ, my parents shared God's Word, and Joy and Pauline sang duets. I didn't join my older sisters because I giggled too much. My responsibility was selling books. Over the next several years, our family held extensive campaigns in Australia's east coastal cities, and many Australians

Chapter Nine: Traveling, Tents, and Caravans

found freedom from guilt and despair as they accepted Christ as their Savior and Lord.

We did have some adventures. Travelling with two vehicles, equipment, and our home-on-wheels was an ongoing challenge. Very few people lived in the Australian outback beyond the main coastal cities, so back-country roads often had major potholes. One day while Mother carefully maneuvered our station wagon around several mega-craters, we noticed a caravan that looked just like ours wandering by itself past us.

It not only looked like our caravan but was! Having somehow disconnected itself from the truck's ball-hitch, it careened through a farmer's fence and up to the farmhouse kitchen window. The farmer's wife was washing dishes when she saw the caravan heading towards her. Dismayed, she ran outside shouting. Beyond the damage, she was worried someone was inside the caravan and might be hurt.

Apologetically, my parents offered to pay for the repair of the fence. The farmer's wife kindly served us hot tea and biscuits while Dad did a makeshift repair to hook the caravan back to the truck, which served until we arrived at a garage for rewelding.

By this point, my sisters had completed their education, attending a total of ten different schools with different curriculums. Since we were now constantly travelling, I enrolled in the Australian National Correspondence School, designed for outback children who couldn't access a school. I received and returned schoolwork through the mail.

Dad saw a great need for ministry in Sydney, Australia's largest city. Selling the tent and equipment, he bought a house in Sydney so we three girls could work while helping plant two churches in outlying suburbs. During post-WW2 years, Australia's government was offering attractive incentives to immigrants from the European continent in particular to increase Australia's sparse population and fill the many employment vacancies. The churches my parents planted were filled with these recently-arrived immigrants, many with stories of unbelievable persecution and hardships.

At fourteen, I completed my basic education. Mother also taught me to type and to write in shorthand, since these secretarial tools had provided her with profitable employment in the Bank of London. Thanks to her encouragement, lots of practice, and patience, I was able to find work as a secretary in a nearby accounting company.

The position was definitely on-the-job training. When my boss asked me to post the accounting books, the only posting I knew of was the mail since mailmen were referred to as postmen. Rather than updating the large ledgers he handed me, I mailed them to our head office.

As I gained experience and confidence, I was offered a higher-paying secretarial position at Exide Battery Company on Sydney's north shore. I rode two trains to my new office location. After work one day, I ran down to the platform since my train was about to leave.

I heard the whistle blow as the train jerked forward. I thought I could still jump on, so I grabbed the steel pole inside the moving carriage. But as the train gained speed toward a tunnel beneath the Sydney Harbor, I was unable to bring my whole body inside to safety. My one leg and foot remained outside, trying to keep up.

Thankfully, someone saw my dilemma and pulled the emergency cord. The entire train jerked to a halt. Embarrassed, I jumped off the train, climbed back to the platform, and found a seat on which to calm down. I never again tried to jump onto a moving train. Thank God for His protection!

I was fifteen when our parents sold our Sydney home to travel again in ministry. For the next several months, we three girls stayed in a boarding house. One day, I went downstairs to the laundry room to wash clothes. An older male resident started conversing with me. Suddenly, he picked me up in his arms and started heading outside to his car, which was parked nearby.

Thankfully, at this moment my sister Pauline appeared. Loudly, she ordered, "You put my sister down!"

Her intervention allowed me to jerk out of the man's tight grip. I will always be thankful for my brave, protective sister. Not long after this, Mother expressed strongly that we should move to England and meet our extended families for the first time. Dad had a long-standing invitation to pastor the congregation in Portsmouth, England, where he'd first been discipled in his faith as a young Christian businessman. Dad accepted Mother's strong conviction and the invitation. At sixteen years old, I said goodbye to the continent that had been my home for the last thirteen years.

Chapter Ten

Goodbye Australia

My parents booked passage on a ship named *Iberia* for the five of us. The trip north through the Gulf of Aden, Red Sea, Suez Canal, Mediterranean Sea, then up the coast of Europe to England would take a total of six weeks. Friends gathered at the docks to see us off as we boarded our ship.

At that time, it was a custom for ship passengers to throw long, multi-colored crepe-paper streamers down to well-wishers on shore as a *bon voyage*. When the ship pulled away, both sides held on to the colorful ribbons until distance finally caused them to break. To me, this was symbolic that we were leaving part of our hearts behind in the land down under.

We enjoyed some good family vacation time on the trip, including stops at numerous interesting ports such as Ceylon, now Sri Lanka, where we visited missionary friends, and Port Said, Egypt, where we mounted camels and purchased leather goods. Approaching the island of Malta, our ship anchored in open seas. We three girls were excited to investigate this island where the apostle Paul had ministered, so we joined other passengers in climbing down ladders into small boats that took us to shore.

Chapter Ten: Goodbye Australia

Wandering through narrow cobblestone streets, we admired many sixteenth-century stone buildings, cathedrals, and palaces.

When we'd finished exploring, we boarded another boat together with several other fellow passengers and paid our fare to return to our ship. The waves had become turbulent and angry, tossing the little boat around. The helmsman waited until we were out on the rough water to demand that we all pay much more than previously agreed. We were at his mercy and desperate to return to our floating home before its loud horn sounded for departure. Thankfully, we scrounged up enough local currency among all of us to satisfy the deceptive helmsman. We were greatly relieved to reach the *Iberia* and climb back on board.

Passing through the Strait of Gibraltar and seeing the magnificent Rock of Gibraltar was another highlight. After six weeks on the high seas, we finally arrived in England. My parents had told us girls many stories of their homeland over the years. But my first impressions were as gloomy as the thick fog outside. Bombed-out buildings, fire damage, and other sad devastation from World War II could be seen everywhere, and we heard many heart-breaking stories of grief and suffering.

But it didn't take long for me to begin enjoying the English culture, pastoral landscape, and quaint architecture as well as getting to know our extended family. Both sets of grandparents had passed away, but we met numerous aunts, uncles, and cousins. One cousin, Vera Gee, was married to the son of Rev. Donald Gee, a well-known Pentecostal Bible teacher in England and author of the popular history of the Pentecostal movement *Wind and Flame*.

Dad bought a house for the family to settle in, and my sisters and I soon found employment. For a short time, Dad pastored the Portsmouth congregation where he'd grown spiritually after finding Christ. But we hadn't been in England long before T.L. and Daisy Osborn again invited my parents to minister with them in evangelistic conferences, this time in Japan and Taiwan. After the conferences, my parents returned to ministry commitments in England. The Osborns stopped to visit us on their own way home to the United States. My sisters and I enjoyed conversing with this dynamic couple.

"Girls, you need to come to the United States," T.L. urged us. "We'll help by sponsoring you. We'll rent an apartment, and you can work in our Tulsa, Oklahoma, headquarters. Your parents can help us in conference ministry based out of England."

Thrilled at this new opportunity, we three girls all applied for American resident visas and were placed on a waiting list. It was about a year later when we finally received our visas. Resigning our work positions, we said farewell to our extended family and boarded a jet airplane headed to New York City. We were on our way to learn a new culture, new currency, new food, new driving patterns on the right-hand side of the road, and a new dialect of English.

My sisters and I arrived in New York on March 8, 1957. My sister Joy was twenty-one, Pauline twenty, and I was seventeen. Upon arrival, we discovered that our connecting flight to Tulsa, Oklahoma, had been cancelled. The next flight wasn't until the following day, so we took a taxi to a nearby hotel. We paid the fee, carefully examining each dollar bill of this new currency, while

Chapter Ten: Goodbye Australia

a uniformed man kindly took our three suitcases. Escorting us to our room, he put down the suitcases and extended his hand.

We each shook his hand and said, "God bless you sir. Many thanks!"

Only much later did we discover that he'd extended his hand in expectation of a tip, a custom completely foreign to us. That was just the first of many new and strange experiences in this strange new country. When we finally made it to Tulsa, the Osborn family took us out to a restaurant, where they ordered fried chicken, a great treat for us. We were immediately horrified when they picked up their chicken pieces with their hands and proceeded to eat them. They in turn undoubtedly thought we were odd as we struggled to eat our chicken with knives and forks.

We left the few possessions we'd brought at the furnished apartment the Osborns had rented for us, then walked to the closest grocery store to purchase basic food items, including a packet of tea and orange juice. The young man who'd bagged the groceries helped us carry them back to our apartment.

We were startled when he looked around and asked, "Where's the baby?"

Once we made clear we were unmarried, he explained, "I assumed you had a baby since you bought baby orange juice."

We'd thought the tiny bottle of juice was orange extract intended to be diluted with water. We were equally surprised when we opened the packet of tea to find only a few individual bags with tea inside instead of a box filled with loose tea. I tore open several tea bags to collect enough tea leaves for a single pot of tea.

Once we'd cashed our first paycheck, we decided to take a bus into the city to shop. We located the bus stop, but waited on the wrong side of the street—i.e., not the right side! Eventually, we learned our way around and found prices quite inexpensive compared to England. After six months, we bought our first car. Pauline was our intrepid chauffeur bravely driving on the "wrong" side of the road.

Now that we had transportation, we were anxious to experience another novelty of American culture—the drive-in restaurant. Reviewing the menu on a screen, we decided to try pizza. We spoke into what we thought was a telephone but turned out to be the heating system. A girl in uniform came out to show us how to order. Returning to her post, she called, "Order, please! Order, please!"

"We would like a pizza," we told her, pronouncing the word as it read phonetically with short "i" and sibilant "z".

"Excuse me?" she interrupted. "What would you like?"

"A pi-zuh," we repeated.

'I'm sorry, I don't think we have that."

"Oh, yes you do! We can see it on the menu screen."

"Then please spell what you are ordering," the attendant responded.

Slowly we spelled pizza: "p-i-zed-zed-a."

The attendant still had no clue what we wanted. We eventually realized we'd not only mispronounced the word pizza but had spelled it the English way with *zed*, not *zee*. Giving up, we left without any food. The next day we told our coworkers about our unsuccessful drive-in restaurant experience. They laughed, explaining that pizza is pronounced "peet-sah," not "pi-zuh." Another lesson learned!

After I'd worked for several months at the Osborns' ministry headquarters, T.L. and Daisy invited me to travel with them around the United States as their secretary and reporter for the magazine *Faith Digest*. One day when I was ordering lunch in a rural Texan restaurant, the waitress noticed my accent.

"How long have you been in America?" she asked.

"About six months," I responded.

"Really!" she exclaimed. "You're doing wonderfully with the English language. I could never learn another language that fast!"

I didn't even try to explain.

The Osborns had recently held meetings in Nigeria, Africa, where they'd documented on film a cruel ritual that involved the village witchdoctor cutting various lines into a newborn's flesh, then rubbing charcoal into the wound to create a pattern of facial scars villagers considered part of their tribal identity as well as protection against evil spirits.

The purpose behind the documentary was to demonstrate visually the drastic change Christ makes in a life, family, and community. I helped with editing the raw footage and found it hard to sleep at night after viewing the graphic scenes and agonized cries of mother and baby. The finished documentary was titled *Black Gold*, denoting the value of each human being, and was premiered in major cities across the country. I was unprepared for the negative reaction from many viewers.

"We are educated people here in the United States! We don't need to see this kind of violence!" I heard routinely and similar sentiments. My eighteen-year-old-heart reacted angrily. After all, if such atrocities were daily occurrences in parts of our world, then shouldn't we need to be aware of the value of each human created in God's image and reach them with Christ's good news?

I was amazed at the many contrasting landscapes, cultures, and racial attitudes across the vast country of the United States. I'd been too young when I lived in British colonial India to be aware of racial discrimination there and hadn't been exposed to racism in Australia. In some southern American cities, local conference organizers planned for a white audience to listen first to the Osborns' message. Only then would people of color be allowed to enter the stadium or other conference venue.

With their compassionate hearts for all cultures and colors, T. L. and Daisy insisted on ministering first to the colored crowd outside and then to the whites inside. I loved seeing how they publicly and privately favored those who were disrespected and mistreated.

Chapter Eleven

Eastern Bible Institute

Years earlier, my parents had been invited by the president of Eastern Bible Institute, now University of Valley Forge, an Assemblies of God academic institution not far from Philadelphia in southeastern Pennsylvania, to speak at their annual spiritual renewal week. Mother had later told us three girls, "If God ever directs you to attend college, your father and I hope it would be Eastern Bible Institute."

After two years fulfilling our obligation to the Osborns, who had so generously sponsored us coming to the United States, my sister and I were ready to write another chapter in our lives. My oldest sister Joy had married a fine Ukrainian minister she'd met in Australia, and together they were pastoring a Ukrainian congregation in Canada.

I was now nineteen years old, and my sister Pauline was twenty-one. We applied for missionary kids scholarships to Eastern Bible Institute and were accepted for the 1958-1959 freshmen class. As we arrived in Pennsylvania, I was reminded of England with its neat row houses and residents speaking a very different accent than that of Oklahoma.

Pauline and I had been out of school working as secretaries for several years, so we were concerned whether we could qualify academically. But our fears abated when we easily passed the incoming English exams. The professors excused our British spelling, and students kindly befriended us. Pauline and I both worked as faculty secretaries, and we enjoyed everything about this new world—studying the Bible, praying in solitude and in groups, being challenged in Friday night mission services, developing lasting friendships, and having fun.

By this point, I'd already dated several young men. In fact looking back, I might admit I was a bit of a flirt. One day while in line to enter the campus dining hall, I noticed a young man who seemed sad. Initiating a conversation, I discovered he wasn't sad, just serious in personality with a strong commitment to eventually serve God in Africa.

My heart's desire was also to reach those without access to God's good news, so it seemed logical this young man could be God's plan for me. We began dating. Later when my parents visited Pauline and me on campus, I introduced them to the young man. After the conversation, Dad whispered, "Hilda, if you wait, God has someone better for you."

I trusted my father's discernment. I also concluded that if Dad was right about God having someone better for me, then God also had someone better for this young man. We broke off our relationship. He later married a classmate, and they loved and served the Lord together. He and his wife continue to be great friends of my husband and me to the present day.

Chapter Eleven: Eastern Bible Institute

On a later visit to EBI, my parents were living out of their station wagon since they were ministering across eastern United States and didn't maintain a home of their own. They had stopped on their drive to campus to purchase postage stamps in a downtown Philadelphia post office. While they were in the post office, thieves broke into the car and stole their clothing, typewriter, and ministry supplies as well as other personal items.

Arriving on campus, my parents shared the sad news with Pauline and me. When I entered my dorm room, I briefly mentioned the loss to my roommate Esther. She was on her way to a missions committee meeting led by Bob Mumford, a senior at EBI who in later decades would become globally known as an outstanding Bible teacher and Christian author. The committee knew my parents since they'd spoken in EBI mission chapels, so Esther shared with the others what had happened.

The students wanted to help my parents but had no idea of the value of their loss. Together they prayed that God would guide them as to the amount they should give the Groves. On separate slips of paper, each wrote an amount. When the treasurer reviewed the slips, he discovered that all five had written the same amount of five hundred dollars.

Bob Mumford commented, "This is the first time I've experienced God speaking to a committee!"

My parents left campus thanking God for supplying the resources to replace their basic needs.

My sister Pauline and I greatly enjoyed our studies and dorm life at EBI. During this time, I discovered a talent for writing as I prepared a series of devotionals from the Old Testament poetic books as an English assignment. Another treasured value of my time at Eastern Bible Institute was developing friendships with other students who have continued to enrich my life through the years.

One such student was classmate Don Wilkerson, whose older brother David became well-known for founding Teen Challenge, a ministry to those seeking freedom from life-controlling issues, as well as Times Square Church in New York City. David had felt called by God to drive from his rural Pennsylvania church to New York City and share God's good news with teen gang leaders.

When we saw press releases with photos of this country preacher, Bible in hand, appealing in court on behalf of these gang leaders, many EBI students thought David's love for these young convicts outweighed wisdom, bringing shame to Jesus Christ. We were totally wrong. David's loving testimony and prayers became the platform to gain the confidence of these gang leaders so he could share Christ's transforming power.

The story of how David Wilkerson led to Christ feuding gang leaders Nicki Cruz and Victor Torres, still top Christian evangelists today, was told in the bestselling book and movie *The Cross and the Switchblade.* Years later, my husband Bill and I were blessed to support this effective ministry from its initial training center in Rehrsburg, PA, as well as in Latin America.

Another classmate named Ed had endured multiple negative foster-home experiences that scarred his life until he found hope and salvation in Christ. One day while a student at EBI, Ed was walking in downtown Philadelphia when he heard gospel music coming from a hotel. Entering, he traced the music to a large room where people were seated in a circle around a small table where a woman sat with a crystal ball. They were singing Christian choruses, but the name Jesus was replaced by Father Divine.

Father Divine was an African-American spiritual leader who claimed to be God. Based in Philadelphia, this cult was at its height in the fifties to mid-sixties. EBI students had been warned about this false teacher and cautioned not to attend any of his group meetings. But Ed's curiosity overruled his caution, and he joined the circle.

Using the crystal ball, the female diviner shared past and future details of each individual listener. Ed felt increasingly uncomfortable at the thought that she might be able to share his traumatic past with everyone in this room. But when the diviner came to Ed, she looked at him, then into the crystal ball, and hesitated.

"Why are you here?" she questioned. "Who are you?"

When Ed didn't respond, she said quietly, "Sir, people's lives are usually transparent to me. This has never happened before, but all I see in you is a red smudge."

Jumped up from his seat, Ed immediately raised his hands in the air and declared, "Thank you, Jesus! Your blood cleanses me from all sin!"

When Ed returned to campus, he shared his experience with my sister and me. Together we affirmed the power of Christ's precious shed blood to give us eternal, abundant life. Ed never went back to that group, and in time he became a spiritual leader whose ministry blessed countless people.

Another classmate who became a life-long friend was Don Kroah, who along with my husband Bill formed part of the Kingsmen Quartet, which represented EBI in camps and churches across eastern United States. Radio had always fascinated Don. After graduating from EBI, he balanced pastoral ministry with a ministry in Christian radio that led to the popular *Don Kroah Show*, which has received many broadcasting awards. He also founded *Reach Africa Now, Inc.* to help equip African pastors and build educational and medical facilities in Africa. Decades later when I became a teacher at our alma mater, now University of Valley Forge, I was privileged to have Don to share in my intercultural communication classes about how God fulfilled his child-hood dream of reaching people through radio.

The summer after our freshman year, Pauline and I had no place to live since our parents didn't own a home and travelled full-time in ministry. A couple in a church where my parents had ministered heard of our need and invited us to live with them during the summer break. Pauline and I both found jobs. Later, the Kingsmen Quartet led by the EBI music director Rev. Robert Krempels sang at that church. After the service, they prayed that God would provide finances for my sister and me to return to school. God answered that prayer but in a different manner than I expected.

"Hilda, you return to school," Pauline told me. "I'll continue to work and help with your expenses."

Chapter Twelve

Physical and Spiritual Giant

Of all the friends God brought into my life at EBI, one stood out above all others, a deep friendship that would permanently change the course of my life. At the beginning of my second academic year at EBI, I was assigned as secretary to the yearbook editor, a tall, thin young man named Bill Bradney.

I was stunned sometime later when a male classmate and good friend informed me that Bill was interested in me. Though Bill was in our class, I saw him as a giant physically and spiritually since he led the Latin America prayer group, sang baritone in the Kingsmen Quartet, and was in general greatly admired and popular. He was also two years older than me as he hadn't started his EBI studies straight out of high school. I didn't feel I deserved the interest of such a highly respected man.

But Bill and I soon became good friends as we worked together on the yearbook. Though he was one of the tallest and I one of the shortest students on campus, our hearts bonded. On our first official date, I knew that one day I would be his wife.

Bill was the oldest child of a hard-working, God-fearing family in western Pennsylvania, where his dad worked on the railroad as a crane driver. Three days after his birth, his parents took their baby across the road to a small church called Gospel Tabernacle. There was no scheduled service, but the young couple walked up to the platform and laid Baby Bill on the altar, dedicating their son to God for His service.

Bill grew up with many happy childhood memories, including events that clearly demonstrated God was watching over him. The three Bradney children had a black cat named Boots they loved very much. They also had an elderly neighbor who despised cats. Boots kept getting sick, and one day the family discovered the neighbor had been feeding Boots poison.

Not wanting to cause a rift with this neighbor, Dad Bradney called a family pow-wow. He'd spoken to a railroad coworker who lived on a farm and had agreed to care for Boots. With sad hearts, the family all agreed that Boots would be safer and happier living in this coworker's barn. Months passed, but Boots was not forgotten.

Then on Christmas Eve when Bill was twelve, his brother Norm ten, and sister Kathy six, the family was gathered in the living room around a brightly-lit Christmas tree. Gifts under the tree waited to be unwrapped the next morning. Inside all was warm and cozy, but outside a blinding blizzard beat against their frame house. Suddenly, the front door rattled loudly.

"Billy, please go check that the front door is tightly closed," asked Dad Bradney.

When Bill opened the door, he saw Boots perched on the front step. She was cold and wet from the snow but healthy and plump. The Bradneys had no idea how she had braved a fourteen mile trek in the middle of a winter blizzard to return to her loving family. Did she somehow know the unkind neighbor had died and the new neighbors were an animal-loving family? The Bradney siblings still recall Boots's return as the best childhood Christmas gift God ever sent them.

The next year thirteen-year-old Bill participated in a Boy Scouts running competition along a country road. Unhappy about the nearby Boy Scouts camp, a disgruntled local farmer had strung barbed wire across the road. Focused on the uneven ground, Bill didn't see the danger and ran full-speed into the wire. Bill crash-landed, the sharp barbs ripping into his face while his top front teeth were knocked out.

The Scout leader rushed Bill to a nearby doctor and advised his parents. Hours of surgery followed. When he returned home with bandaged face, his dad gathered the family for a discussion. The family had been advised to take legal action against the farmer, but Dad Bradney decided they would instead pray.

First, they gave thanks that the barbed wire had not cut any main arteries in Bill's neck. Then they prayed for healing. If God healed Bill's face with no visible scars, the family wouldn't take legal action but allow the local authorities to deal with the farmer's illegal actions.

What a celebration when the doctor removed the bandages and discovered healthy new skin. Dentures were made to replace Bill's upper front teeth, and remaining scars were only visible to dentists. Thanks, Dad Bradney, for showing us that trusting God is the high road.

Throughout high school, Bill was an honor student. He also enjoyed playing basketball. He and his brother Norm earned pocket money picking wild blackberries, mowing lawns, and delivering newspapers. When Bill turned fifteen, his dad gave him a newspaper highlighting three want-ads. "Billy, check out these work opportunities."

Bill found a job in a dry-cleaning plant after school and on Saturdays. His dad further instructed, "Ten percent of your salary belongs to God, fifty percent is for your upkeep, and forty percent is for yourself."

Bill thought this was unfair at first, but later he was thankful since his dad saved the fifty percent upkeep portion to help finance his son's future college expenses. Bill eventually left the dry-cleaning job to sell retail shoes, then was offered a good-paying position in the accounting department of IBM.

From childhood, Bill had a deep desire to know God. While the Bradney family attended a Methodist church, Bill often attended a nearby Baptist church Sunday evenings on his own. After a family move, the entire family attended a local Baptist church, and Bill enjoyed playing on their youth basketball team.

But once he was in junior high, peer pressure cooled Bill's spiritual hunger as he tried to blend in with his party-going school friends. That said, when friends offered Bill a cigarette, he remembered vividly his decision as a ten-year-old when a guest speaker had shared the dangers of smoking with his Sunday school class. The speaker had given each student a card to sign that read: "God helping me, I will not smoke and contaminate my body that God created for His glory." Bill had signed the card and remained faithful to that pledge.

Bill was seventeen when one of his dad's coworkers invited the Bradneys to revival meetings in their hometown. The preacher's message, "Elevator to Hell," described eternal loss for those who reject God's gift of salvation. Bill was deeply convicted of having drifted from his former close walk with God. When an invitation was given to make peace with God, Bill rushed to the altar. His mom, dad, brother, and sister joined him there, and the entire family experienced life-transformation as they knelt in submission to the Lordship of Christ. That night, Bill promised God that he would love and serve Him each day of his life.

From that point, the entire family grew spiritually. Under Bill's high school graduation yearbook photo, his classmates described him as timid and a man of few words. But as Bill matured in his faith, he was elected leader of his church youth group. His leadership qualities developed, and he wanted to serve God wherever He would lead him. When a new pastor came to their church, he introduced himself to Bill, then said, "Young man, God has His hand on your life for full-time service. You should attend Bible School to prepare yourself."

Bill was grateful and humbled that God would call him. He resigned his job at IBM and enrolled in the freshman class of 1957-1958 at Eastern Bible Institute. IBM was a booming company and Bill was a valued employee, so he anticipated that his supervisor would try to dissuade him from leaving. Instead, his supervisor congratulated Bill for his decision to invest his life in serving others and gave Bill a sizeable check to help pay his college expenses.

Chapter Thirteen

The Hill-Billy Team

Before coming to EBI, Bill had already prayed to God about his future wife, jotting down a list of characteristics he wanted in his wife. He also committed to reserving his first kiss for the woman he would marry.

Once at EBI, Bill quickly adjusted to campus life, enjoying Bible study, new friends, and opportunities to serve, including leading the Latin America prayer band, helping organize Friday night mission chapels, editing the yearbook, and singing with the Kingsmen Quartet. He also worked part-time in a nearby furniture factory. In my second year of studies, my relationship with Bill had developed into strong friendship as we shared mutual goals and willingness to obey God wherever, whenever, to whoever.

During the following spring break, Bill's family invited me to visit their home. Bill had purchased a car from a classmate for fifty dollars. As we drove across Pennsylvania, I encountered my first blinding snowstorm. Then the car hood flew up in front of us. Thankfully, we didn't crash, and Bill found a metal coat hanger to fasten the hood into place.

At his home, I was warmly welcomed by Bill's wonderful parents and siblings. His sister Kathy informed Bill, "Brother, if you don't marry this girl, I will disown you!"

Chapter Thirteen: The Hill-Billy Team

That didn't prove necessary as by the end of that visit Bill had proposed to me, followed by our first kiss. We were growing more and more deeply in love and walking on air as we began thinking and dreaming of a future together.

During their time touring in ministry across eastern United States, my parents planted a church in Shillington, Pennsylvania. They still had no home of their own, so when I finished my second year at EBI, I left school to help them remodel a brick hall on the church property into a parsonage and small apartment for travelling evangelists and missionaries. I also worked part-time in an insurance agency.

During construction, Dad, Mother, and I camped in the church basement. One morning we awoke to find our basement home floor flooded with water from a heavy downpour. But despite such adventures, the church grew, and God blessed my parents' ministry.

I'd dreamed of becoming formally engaged on my twenty-first birthday. Bill had now graduated as EBI was a three-year program, but he had already committed to the Kingsmen Quartet summer tour. I didn't know he'd already purchased my engagement ring and was secretly carrying it around during the tour. Their last concert was scheduled on my birthday. Around midnight, Bill arrived at our church from his final singing commitment, carrying his treasure.

By now we'd courted for a year. The dark, spooky atmosphere of this old church basement didn't concern us as he slid his ring on my finger, officially sealing our commitment to a life-long relationship. My dream had been fulfilled on my twenty-first birthday, and God's Hil-Billy Team—Hilda and Bill—was now official.

Though I was delighted to be marrying Bill, I didn't want a church wedding with lots of people looking at me. The reason went back to my childhood when Dad asked his three bonnie girls to sing "Are you Washed in the Blood?" at evangelistic services. I've already mentioned my embarrassing problem of giggles. Though my sisters and I started the song as a trio, it concluded as a duet after I began giggling uncontrollably and had to sit down with a red, shamed face.

I continued to giggle right into adulthood whenever I spoke in public. So I much preferred a quiet, intimate family celebration for my wedding. But my parents had made plans to return to India in ministry after the wedding, and Bill had been selected to take their place as pastor of the newly-planted Shillington church. I knew the congregation would expect their new pastor and wife to have a church wedding, so I agreed.

I giggled throughout our wedding rehearsal, totally ashamed of myself. Before bed that night, I prayed, *Dear Jesus, I want you to receive honor and glory in our wedding ceremony, especially since many attending may not know you. Please, Jesus, help me not to giggle.*

The entire wedding party along with my parents prayed together before leaving the parsonage for the older traditional church building where the wedding ceremony was being held. As I entered the sanctuary with its beautiful stained-glass windows, my sister Joy played the ornate pipe organ while Bill sang to me a love song, "Because you are mine!"

God answered our prayer because I wasn't tempted to giggle or even aware of guests staring. As I listened to my bridegroom's beautiful baritone, I felt engulfed in God's sacred presence.

Chapter Thirteen: The Hill-Billy Team

My father and the pastor from Bill's home church shared the wedding ceremony. As Bill and I knelt at the altar, the majestic strains of "The Lord's Prayer" echoed across the sanctuary. Laying his hands on our shoulders, Dad quietly but very clearly spoke prophetic words over us. "If you are faithful to the Lord, He will use you in a unique way to bless multitudes in missions."

Humbled, Bill and I echoed, "Amen, let it be!"

Those were unforgettable words from God. After the ceremony, we all gathered in the church basement that had been our home during construction, which we'd painted the day before the wedding. Family, friends, and church members had brought goodies and fruit punch for the reception. There was also a beautifully decorated wedding cake that had a story of its own.

A dear friend who was a baker, Mabel Hurst, had offered to make my wedding cake. When she asked what kind of cake I wanted, I responded, "Three tiers with pillars holding the top-layer would be wonderful. Our wedding colors are pale-yellow and lavender."

"I've never made a cake with pillars," Mabel informed me, "but let me see what I can do."

Cutting an old wooden broom handle into four pillars, Mable washed and painted them, then covered them with icing to be the pillars holding up the top cake tier. Bill joked later, "Honey, I just swept you off your feet!"

For a wedding dress, I wore the one my sister Joy had used. Invitations, flowers, wedding-party gifts, photos, and those food items we'd purchased for the reception totaled a hundred dollars. Our happy, sacred memories remain priceless!

Chapter Fourteen

A Solid Foundation

For our honeymoon, we borrowed Bill's parents' car and drove up to Camp-of-the-Woods, a Christian family resort, camp, and conference center located on the Finger Lakes in upstate New York. While we were there, the camp was hosting a missions conference for Latin America Mission. We had no idea then that eight years later we'd be serving in Costa Rica alongside many LAM missionaries and that our children would enjoy great fellowship with LAM missionary kids.

From day one of our marriage, we kept in mind our commitment when we got engaged to build our marriage on the strong foundation of God's Word and prayer. Each day, we read a Bible portion together, then asked God's favor and direction for that day. This daily practice definitely contributed to a life-long thriving marriage.

Just two months after my own wedding, Pauline married a young man she'd met while attending Eastern Bible Institute, Halden Curtiss. She looked beautiful in the same wedding dress Joy and I had worn. Over the following years, they pastored several churches in the Northeast before accepting the invitation

Chapter Fourteen: A Solid Foundation

to pastor The Little Brown Church in Bigfork, Montana, where they remained until retirement.

My parents had now returned to India, leaving Bill and I to pastor the Shillington church. For our first Christmas, we struggled as to how we should decorate the parsonage. The adult Sunday School teacher had expressed that a Christmas tree was a pagan practice that didn't honor God. We personally felt the traditional Christmas tree was beautiful with no connections to negative superstitions.

On Christmas Eve when decorations were half-price, Bill and I ended up purchasing a small silver aluminum tree along with festive lights. The cashier totaled the cost: $6.66, the same numbers as ascribed to "the mark of the beast" in the book of Revelation. Bill and I looked at each other, laughing, as the cashier clearly wondered what the joke was. We were glad the adult Sunday School teacher hadn't been there to observe!

That Christmas tree decorated our home for many years in Pennsylvania. Since it folded up easily, the tree went with us to Costa Rica, where it adorned church dramas all over that country.

Bill and I were both hungering to know more of God. Hearing how God was using Kathryn Kuhlman, a well-known Pentecostal evangelist, we visited her meetings, where we witnessed powerful miracles of healing and God's awesome presence. We also visited Saturday evening services led by Rev. James Brown, pastor of Presbyterian Church in Parkesburg, Pennsylvania. People from all denominations and locations crowded the sanctuary for these services, a revival whose impact carried into following generations.

Do Angels Wear Overalls?

In 1962, God blessed us with our first child, a darling blonde baby girl. We named her after my middle name, Ruth, and her Grandma Bradney, Annette. The Sunday after Ruth's birth, we were anxious to show our church family God's sweet gift. I was still too big for my normal clothes, so I decided to wear a maternity dress with a belt.

As was his custom, Bill walked to the church early. It took longer than anticipated to get both myself and baby Ruth ready. Then I carefully descended the parsonage steps with Ruth in my arms. Worshippers were already arriving, and several people hurried over to admire our newborn.

As I walked, I felt something falling. *No, it can't be! Yes, it is!* I took bigger steps, but it didn't help. In front of many onlookers, my pregnancy-stretched underpants fell down over my shoes. Slowly, I stepped out of them, leaving a puddle of white material on the green lawn.

Just at that moment, Bill came around the corner of the church, looking for me since I was to play the pipe organ. As he grasped what he was seeing, his face turned bright-red. Quickly, he took baby Ruth while I stooped down, picked up my panties, and returned home.

There I found a safety pin, which I used to shorten the frayed elastic that had stretched a few days earlier over my very pregnant stomach. I then returned sheepishly to church where I walked down the side aisle past our dear parishioners and hid behind the pipe organ, embarrassed beyond words.

I decided then that if our daughters grew up to marry and have children, my first practical gift to them would be new underwear!

My parents didn't remain in India long. After they returned to the Shillington church, Bill resigned to take a small rural church in James City, Pennsylvania. We lived in a rented apartment above a dress shop twenty-five miles from the church and received twenty-five dollars a week from the church. We were grateful as we knew it was all the congregation could afford to give. But it wasn't enough to cover basic needs for three people.

Still, Bill, baby Ruth, and I never went hungry, and God helped us remain current with rent, car payment, utilities, gas, groceries, etc. One morning we found a sack of potatoes at the foot of the stairs with a note that read: *I don't know you, but felt you needed these. Enjoy!*

Then one day about two years after we'd moved to the James City church, everything changed. The night Bill proposed, we'd promised each other that whenever a problem arose, we would pray asking for divine wisdom to resolve it. But this time we broke that promise, making a quick, bad decision without asking God's guidance.

An Assemblies of God home missions representative who'd been assigned to us as a new AG ministry couple in the area stopped by unexpectedly. Plopping onto our couch, he explained the purpose of his visit. "Bill and Hilda, I know you are struggling financially. I have God's answer for you."

Eagerly, we sat on the edge of our kitchen chairs as he showed us a list of other Christian leaders and colleagues who had entered the plan. "Here is how this works. You only need twenty-five dollars investment to enter the ground floor of a pyramid. Then you visit seven friends, asking them to pledge the same. They will each then find seven friends to invest, and so on. With each additional investor, you rise up the pyramid. When you reach the highest level, you'll receive a landfall!"

Of course we knew nothing of pyramid marketing or how such schemes work as this was very brand-new at that time. Our doubts were quickly brushed aside as our mentor insisted that this totally legal plan was God's way to subsidize our meager income. We'd just received our weekly check for twenty-five dollars. We reluctantly signed it over to our mentor, leaving us with a zero bank balance.

Immediately, we felt uneasy. A few difficult weeks passed. There was no anonymous gift of potatoes or unexpected note with a gift inside or other answer to our prayers. Nor was there any good communication between Bill and me. We realized we'd disobeyed God in entering this pyramid scheme. We were both discouraged and desperate. Finally, I called my dear parents. With tears, I confessed our disobedience.

"Hilda, you knew that wasn't right!" Dad's shocked voice blurted. He prayed with Bill and me. Later he called back. "Bill and Hilda, the congregation here loves you both and often talk about the blessing you were for the two years you were here. I feel called to return to India. Would you return to Shillington and pastor this congregation along with your mother?"

A ray of hope and forgiveness beamed into our dark feelings of defeat and shame. We sadly said goodbye to church families we'd grown to love, sold our used furniture and refrigerator to fill our car's gas tank, and headed back to Shillington.

Chapter Fourteen: A Solid Foundation

My parents and their growing congregation graciously welcomed back Bill, Ruth, and me. Two weeks later, our Assemblies of God general superintendent sent out a pastoral letter detailing the involvement of AG ministers and leaders in eastern USA in an illegal financial scandal. Distressed and disappointed, he proceeded to say that AG headquarters would not hinder any legal charges against the participants. Bill and I were ashamed of our gullibility but also grateful we hadn't pressured friends to participate.

For the next year, Bill worked with the church as his day job and at a gasoline station at night to pay outstanding bills from our former location. This painful experience taught us a most important life lesson. When we were later invited into dubious business opportunities overseas, we immediately remembered our big blunder and continued to trust God as our Provider as we served Him full-time.

Chapter Fifteen

Growing Church and Family

Bill and I were delighted to discover I was pregnant with our second child. Philip was born with auburn hair and a fun personality. Wherever we went, his red-gold hair color attracted compliments and even touching. This made him self-conscious, especially once we were in Costa Rica where most people had black hair. After he reached his teens, he began to enjoy the attention his unusual hue received from the opposite gender.

A family of four made it a challenge to budget our small income. But the reward of seeing lives forgiven and flourishing was our paycheck, and God met our needs in meaningful ways as we sought to honor Him.

Whenever possible, we invited missionaries to share their stories and needs with us and our congregation. After one New Zealand missionary couple, the Browns, who served in Papua, New Guinea, shared in a Sunday evening service, Bill was deeply impacted. Without sharing his plans with me, he put our entire week's salary in their missions offering. This was not like Bill, and he was most apologetic. But I supported him since he felt this was

Chapter Fifteen: Growing Church and Family

what God wanted, though I did wonder how we would cover our ongoing living expenses for that week.

The following Wednesday after the evening Bible Study, a faithful church member appropriately nicknamed Sister Smiley unexpectedly handed Bill an envelope. When we opened it, we found double the amount Bill had given in the Sunday evening offering. It was designated for our personal use. Together we thanked God.

Another morning, we heard a knock on the parsonage front door. Outside we found Robert Nagle, a boy who attended our church with his sister and parents, standing there with a big smile and a large red tomato on a paper plate.

"Wow, Robert, what a lovely tomato!" I exclaimed.

Bill and I were rather speechless at this most unusual gift. Coming inside, Robert explained: "Pastor Bill, I planted my first garden this spring, and this is my first tomato. I want to give my first fruit to God!"

We took a photo of Robert's tomato, then prayed over him, thanking God for the tomato and asking God to bless and guide this precious child. Decades later while on furlough from Latin America, we spoke at a church that had faithfully supported our ministry. We'd heard the Nagle family was attending there, so after the service we asked the lead pastor about them.

"Oh, yes, Robert is our wonderful treasurer," the pastor replied. "He has faithfully served this congregation for many years."

My mind immediately went to that scene with the "first-fruit" tomato. Mom and Dad Nagle had faithfully planted good seed in the tender soil of their son's heart, and we were privileged to witness some of the resulting fruit. Robert's precious wife Wendy eventually went on to serve Global Disciples, an organization that trains workers who disciple and plant churches among today's least-reached people groups around the world.

Bill and I received an invitation to pastor a small rural congregation outside Titusville, Pennsylvania, where the American oil industry was birthed. In 1965, we resigned from the Shillington congregation and advised the Titusville congregation that we'd accept their kind invitation on the condition that as God blessed we move the church into the city. The original church was located next to a junk yard in the outlying township of Moss Grove, so in fun we sang the old hymn, "There's a church in the valley by the junk yard."

We were always delighted to have my mother visit us and her two grandchildren. One morning Mother and I were enjoying a mother-daughter moment when the telephone rang. I answered it in the living room, so I didn't see Mother reach across the gas stove to the whistling kettle to make a cup of tea. Mother was unaware that her polyester dress had brushed the gas flame and caught on fire.

Just then, Bill walked in the house and saw Mother's dress burning. He immediately went into action beating out the fire with his bare hands. He screamed and danced in pain as the melting polyester burnt his hands. Turning, I saw Bill's bizarre behavior. Why was he hitting at my dear mother?

Then I realized what was happening. Hanging up the phone, I rushed over to turn off the gas stove. We quickly extinguished the fire. Mother's dress had a gaping hole, and her hair was singed, but

Chapter Fifteen: Growing Church and Family

the fire had thankfully not reached her tender skin. As we processed what had happened, we recognized God's intervention in bringing Bill home at the very moment Mother caught on fire. We thanked God for His perfect timing and Bill's quick rescue.

My dad had once again returned stateside from India. In 1965, my parents both felt it was time to return there together. This was a sad farewell as Mother suffered with Parkinson's disease, and we knew our next reunion with Mother might be in heaven. Dad bought an Airstream trailer and a Chevy station wagon, which he had shipped to France. They then drove this home-on-wheels from France to India. This proved quite an adventure, but they eventually arrived safely in Bangalore, India. They lived in the Airstream in Bangalore for several years.

We were now a family of four and enjoyed serving the Titusville congregation. Bill served as secretary to the local ministerium, and we enjoyed great fellowship with our leaders and colleagues. One Sunday evening, a new group of people joined us in worship. They shared that the American Baptist Society was about to close their church because it couldn't support a full-time pastor. They wondered if we'd hold an early Sunday morning service at their church before our own service, a Thursday night Bible Study, and other pastoral responsibilities.

Our Assemblies of God district superintendent gave us his blessing. The quaint, white-steepled church changed its name to Chapmanville Community Church. Both congregations grew and became missionary-sending churches. One missionary serving in Japan was supported by the Chapmanville congregation and had been invited to share in their Thursday evening service. He'd been given the address to our parsonage but was sure it must be incorrect when he discovered it was on the property of the Moss Grove Assemblies of God church.

We assured him it was indeed the correct address and warmly welcomed him into our little home. He was polite but aloof as though trying to understand how a Baptist church was being pastored by an Assemblies of God pastor. After a home-cooked meal, we gathered with the Chapmanville congregation, where the guest shared slides and spoke of his struggles in Japan. Bill promoted a generous mission offering.

We housed the missionary for the night, fellowshipping over hot chocolate and home-made cookies, then making him comfortable in our children's bedroom. By morning, his formal attitude had completely thawed. The following week, a package arrived containing a beautiful Japanese set of cups with a very warmly-written thank you note.

Our red-headed son Phil added much fun to our little family. In summer 1966 when he was two years old, he was exploring Bill's office chair, swirling it around, pushing it, then sitting in it like his tall dad. When I checked on him, I found a screw on the floor. Two other screws were still in place on the chair, but there were four screw holes.

When I asked Phil where the fourth screw had gone, he pointed to his throat. We rushed him to the hospital. The attending doctor reassuringly patted my shoulder. "Lady, don't worry. If he swallowed the screw, it will most likely come out in his stool. My grandson

Chapter Fifteen: Growing Church and Family

swallowed an open safety pin. We stuffed him with bread to coat the pin, then watched it on X-rays travel right out of his system. Give the boy as much bread as he can eat, and check his stool constantly. If it doesn't appear within three days, bring him back in."

Our challenge was that we were scheduled to leave the next morning to counsel youth at Living Waters Camp, an AG camp facility in a rural area. There was no camp nurse or doctor and only one telephone to serve the entire camp. We gave Phil bread to eat and decided to leave as planned, packing a portable potty-chair. The next morning, we welcomed several hundred youth for camp.

Each morning, the counsellors and staff joined for a brief devotional and prayer time before the camp schedule started. The first morning, Bill shared, "This may be the most unusual request you've ever heard, but we need a miracle. Our two-year-old son has a loose screw! This is day three, and we still haven't yet found the screw in his stool."

The week progressed packed with activities. Each morning, we were questioned, "Have you found the screw?"

"Not yet," we kept answering. Then on day seven, I was checking the contents of the potty-chair when I struck something hard. It was the screw. I screamed in joy and relief. We all were overjoyed. The loose screw had been found!

When Bill and I realized God had surprised us with another pregnancy, we decided to find a hospital near Bill's parents, who welcomed us to their home during what I'd calculated as my last week. When rhythmic pains and pressure mounted, Bill took me to the nearby hospital, but medication and walking failed to induce labor. This was before routine sonograms, and I was embarrassed to discover we'd miscalculated the baby's delivery date by a month!

A month later on a Sunday morning, I knew this time it was the real deal. Bill rushed from the Titusville pulpit to my in-laws' home, and we were off to the hospital. Our VW bug nearly became the delivery room. We arrived at the hospital just in time for my doctor to assist the baby's birth.

As I cradled baby Cheryl Joy in my arms, Bill and I discovered this bundle of joy had auburn hair similar to her four-year-old brother Phil, clearly a recessive trait since neither of her parents had red-hued hair. She was soon surrounded with love and hugs from us all. Her six-year-old sister Ruth helped mother her little sister. We were truly blessed.

Chapter Sixteen

Go and I Will Be With You!

When Bill and I needed to invest more time into our growing Assemblies of God congregation, the Chapmanville Community Church invited Bill's brother Norman to pastor that congregation. We enjoyed pastoring our own congregation and were thrilled when a few of our young people left to train for full-time ministry. Two single women from our congregation also headed to Alaska, where they served two indigenous communities for several decades.

In July 1968, Bill directed the same Living Waters youth camp where our son Phil had his adventure passing a screw. With Cheryl just a month old, I stayed home. One morning during my quiet time with God, I reflected on God's promise at our wedding that one day He'd use Bill and me to bless multitudes in missions. Every time a visiting missionary shared their ministry, I'd been feeling sad that we weren't serving in some part of the world still greatly in need of the gospel. I began talking candidly to God.

Lord, You know that since childhood I've wanted to serve You in missions. We now have three children and will soon be in our thirties. The older we are, the harder it is to learn a new language or be appointed by the Assemblies of God World Missions. You know, Lord, I promised I'd never pressure my husband into missions. That is Your business. But if You want us to serve overseas, would You please confirm that to me and speak to my dear husband? If not, would You please take that desire out of my heart so I can be the happiest pastor's wife in Pennsylvania?

When I finished praying, I randomly opened my Bible. The pages fell open to Exodus 3 where God is speaking to Moses from the burning bush. The following phrases from Exodus 3:10-12 jumped off the pages into my heart: "So now, go. I [God]am sending you . . . Who am I that I should go? . . . And God said, I will be with you." (NIV)

This was a clear word from God. Jumping up, I danced around the room, raising my hands and heart in joyful praise. "Thank You, Jesus! Since You have spoken to me, I know You are speaking to my dear husband as well. I thank You for that too!"

Meanwhile out at Living Waters, Bill was staying busy and blessed directing the youth camp. One morning around 3 a.m., he'd checked that the teens were all in their assigned cabins, then fell into his bunk, exhausted. Suddenly he was wide awake, a clear impression in his heart and mind that God was speaking to him. "Bill, do you remember that morning under the grand piano when I asked if you'd be willing to go should I call you into overseas service?"

Bill remembered the occasion well. There had been an extended move of God among EBI students. During an early morning prayer meeting, the altar area had been so packed with students that Bill had crawled under the grand piano to pray. There he'd heard clearly God's question as to his willingness to follow God into missions.

He also remembered his father-in-law's prophetic words during our wedding ceremony as well as the new pastor at the church he'd attended during his teens who'd told Bill the first time they'd met, "Bill, God's hand is on your life for ministry."

Bill had felt blessed beyond measure that God would choose him as a full-time minister. He'd prayed, "Lord, if you want me to serve you in overseas missions, not just the pastorate, I will obey. But I need to be assured You are the one commissioning me."

Now in this rustic camp cabin, God spoke clearly once again. "I asked you seven years ago if you were willing. Now I'm giving you the green light to go!"

Bill couldn't wait to share God's message with me. When he drove up to the parsonage in our little blue VW bug, I stepped outside to greet him. His face looked radiant as we hugged.

"Sweetheart, I have wonderful news for you!" he burst out.

"Honey, I have even better news for you!" I responded.

As Bill and I shared our conversations with God over the past few days, we discovered that God had affirmed His call to each of us at the very same time though we were miles apart. We were thrilled beyond words. We immediately wrote to give the good news to my parents in India. On August 8, 1968, we received the following response from Dad.

I have been expecting to receive such an intimation from you for a long time. This is just what we expected although it is now getting late in the day . . . Although we [my parents] are only 50% qualified now, we are thankful that we obeyed the Lord coming [back] to India to do at least a little before we meet Him... You [Bill and Hilda] still have a few years, strength, and ministry.

I could read between the lines of his letter that since Dad and Mother had more limited strength in these latter years compared to their earlier service in India and around the world, Dad was feeling that his ministry impact there in Bangalore was less effective. In fact, the opposite was true. Instead of constantly travelling in intense evangelistic services, my parents were ministering locally on a more in-depth basis, and countless people were coming to my parents to receive one-on-one training, counsel, and prayer. Dad went on in his letter:

I will take the liberty of throwing out my personal thoughts for you to sort out. Try to avoid living under the supervision of any missionary couple, however good they may be. Try to avoid being confined to a missionary compound... Your first priority is training national workers... this is the greatest and most urgent need... When in Taiwan Formosa, Africa, Japan, and Poland, we could have spent the rest of our lives preaching to thousands, and we would have been very happy. How thankful we are now here [in Bangalore] to meet urgent needs in

India . . . You must follow your own leadings and be free to develop your own methods and ministry.

That year, Bill asked me what I'd like for Christmas. I told him I'd like to call Mother in India for three minutes, the minimum for an overseas call and at this time very expensive. My sister Pauline and her family were spending Christmas with us. She asked her husband for the same gift, so on Christmas Day my sister and I excitedly called Mother in Bangalore, one of us on a downstairs phone, the other on an upstairs extension.

It had been several years since we'd hugged our goodbyes on their ship in New York City harbor. When Mother answered the phone, her heavy English accent delighted us. Pauline, Mother, and I all started to laugh. Three minutes quickly sped by, and we hadn't conversed, only laughed.

What an expensive Christmas telephone call considering we didn't even speak! I told myself afterwards. But a short time later we received a letter from Mother saying that laughing together had lifted her spirits. We often laughed together so this was a typical Groves gift.

Within a year of our commitment to missions, Bill and I were commissioned, trained, and raising our support funds as Assemblies of God career missionaries. While we didn't feel called to any particular country, Bill was especially burdened for Latin America. At the suggestion of our missions director Dr. Melvin Hodges, we wrote to various Latin American countries that had expressed urgent need for more workers. We prayed over each response. After reading one letter from Costa Rica field director William Brooke, Bill and I both agreed this was where our service was most needed.

At the recommendation of our mission agency, I also applied to become an American citizen. The naturalization ceremony was sacred as well as celebratory as I exchanged the Union Jack for the Stripes and Stars while retaining my true kingdom citizenship.

In 1969 as we prepared to go to Costa Rica, we were blessed to stay at the interdenominational Overseas Ministries Study Center in Ventnor, NJ, just two blocks from the Atlantic Ocean, which provided short-term housing for missionaries who were stateside among its many programs. While Bill travelled to share the need in Costa Rica and raise necessary ministry funds, I worked parttime as secretary to the director and cared for our three children.

One night in November 1969 while Bill was travelling, I felt God's presence draw near in a way that is hard to describe. It felt sacred, holy, as though I was experiencing a taste of heaven. Words seemed unnecessary as I worshiped, cried, and enjoyed God's beautiful presence for several hours.

Early the next morning, I received a telegram from India that read: *Darling Mother with Jesus, Love Dad.* I'd had no possible way to visit my dearly loved mother in India during her last days on earth, but I didn't question God's will. Instead, I gave thanks that the very night she'd passed, God had allowed me to experience a taste of His holy presence that Mother was now enjoying fully.

I learned later that Mother's last words as she ascended into God's presence had been a joyous "Higher, higher, higher!" Even now as I recall these sacred moments, I am wiping away tearful eyes.

Bill and I concluded our first newsletter to supporting churches and prayer partners:

Would you pray for us as we are keenly aware of our need for more of God. We freshly dedicate our lives to Christ and His charge: "As the Father has sent me, so send I you" (John 20:21 TLB).

The Bradney Family leaving for Costa Rica.

Chapter Seventeen

Loving and Learning Costa Rica

Bill and I had never visited Costa Rica and didn't know a soul there. But as we boarded a plane in July 1970 to San Jose, the capital of Costa Rica, we were excited to fulfil our dreams and God's plan. We experienced our first adventure as soon as the flight reached Costa Rica since San Jose and the airport turned out to be locked in by heavy clouds.

The pilot circled around above the city for over half an hour, looking for an opening to land. The wind turbulence felt like a roller-coaster. Most passengers vomited, including myself and two-year-old Cheryl on my lap. Flight attendants couldn't leave their own seats to help. The pilot announced that the flight would be diverting to Panama until the skies cleared. But at the last moment, he found an opening sufficient to dive down onto the runway.

On the ground, we hurried to the restrooms, where I cleaned myself and Cheryl as best I could with toilet paper purchased from the restroom attendant. Once we made it through Immigration and shepherded our luggage through Customs, we found a group of Costa Ricans and North American missionaries waiting to welcome us. The national AG superintendent and our future missionary colleagues all warmly hugged us despite our stained, horrid-smelling clothes.

We were taken to the home of AG field leaders William and Hope Brooke for a welcome dinner at the Brooke's home. Before the meal, their daughter Sylvia kindly exchanged Cheryl's dirty dress for a clean one belonging to a very large doll she had. This became the start of many years learning, growing, serving, loving, and later sending Costa Ricans.

Until we found a house rental, our family stayed in a two-room apartment on the Assemblies of God Bible Institute campus. Some fifty to seventy residential students lived in campus dormitories and ate in the Bible Institute dining hall. One of my first impressions of Costa Rica was the lack of garbage. From our upstairs window, I watched as garbage collectors emptied the school's single barrel of rubbish for that week into an open truck.

"Where is the rest of rubbish?" I asked the school cook Vera.

"That's all," she responded. "The rest is all recycled or used as compost."

This was hard for me to imagine. The weekly waste for this entire campus resembled that of our five-member family back in the United States. Later after we'd moved into our rented house, I would place our garbage can out on the sidewalk for pickup. Within five minutes, any number of people were rummaging through it, trying to find something useful. Nearly everything Americans might throw away was of value to someone. Containers, cans, and boxes were all reused. Automobiles that were twenty and even thirty years old were patched up and still on the roads.

Reflecting on this, I was reminded of Jesus's command to his disciples after miraculously feeding five thousand-plus hungry people with a boy's lunch of bread and fish: "Gather the pieces that are left over. Let nothing be wasted!" (John 6:12 NIV). Apparently, God doesn't waste anything!

The Spanish Language Institute was an interdenominational school that taught Spanish to missionaries and other expatriates serving in Latin America. The only Spanish words Bill and I knew were *sí* (yes) and *no* (no), so we started language school in the beginner's class. Listening, observing, questioning, and laughing at our own blunders filled each day.

Answering the door or telephone always brought risk of humiliation. Ruth was now eight years old, Phil six, and Cheryl two. They learned the basic words much faster than we did and had no concerns over presenting a good image, so they quickly became our answer to that dilemma.

Since we were there as a family, many of our most urgent Spanish-language questions and responses revolved around household needs and shopping. I received a fair amount of practice outside of classes trying to communicate with our household maid and guard. So unintentionally, I soon found myself at the forefront whenever Bill and I were speaking Spanish in public, something I struggled with as I knew this was demoralizing for Bill.

Thankfully, this changed after we graduated. Bill began accompanying experienced missionaries to rural churches, where he was invited to teach Bible messages in Spanish. These country trips reestablished Bill's confidence as the rural believers seemed to have more time and patience to endure a new missionary's butchered Spanglish. With practice, Bill's Spanish vocabulary and phonetics flourished. I was thrilled when he began taking the initiative in Spanish conversations wherever we were. Even now, he enjoys conversing in Spanish.

If the language challenge had knocked us off the foreign missionary/hero pedestal, other subtle pressures nearly shipwrecked us. Not being able to preach or testify made Bill and me feel useless. I couldn't even play the piano for church since most of the Spanish gospel songs had no written music and were sung in minor keys unfamiliar to me.

I also fought guilt over our children. They needed a mother's attention, but our days were packed with classes each morning while afternoons and evenings were spent preparing for the next morning's classes. There was also endless administrative red tape to deal with as foreigners in Costa Rica. Bill reacted physically to the pressure by developing a bleeding ulcer that put him in the hospital.

But we gradually did learn cultural and life-lessons as well as Spanish. Since our Spanish words were limited, we learned to bless others more by actions instead of words. We learned to appreciate and accept understanding support from missionary colleagues and national believers. God's call became an anchor for our tossed-about emotions. Without spiritual nourishment in English, we were forced to dig into God's Word for ourselves.

In summary, we learned that when God sends, His grace sustains. In September 1970, we noted in a ministry newsletter to family and supporting friends:

Deeply entrenched in Spanish language study, we give our best concentrated efforts to this needed tool of expression. Please pray that God will help us. Many adjustments are minor in comparison to our great joy seeing sincerity and hunger for God. Last night ministering to youth, we met a teen converted two months ago. He has already started a branch church. Each service in church buildings, houses, and classrooms has been packed. People sit so close together! Some walked three hours through wooded areas to attend the service from 11 a.m. to 11.30 p.m. They returned home by flashlight with a song in their hearts . . . Yes, it's great to be here!

During our year of language study in 1970, the entire language institute experienced a great spiritual awakening. Cottage prayer meetings among different denominational missionaries sprang up with many receiving power from on high. Most evangelical congregations in San Jose were impacted as well as Roman Catholic churches.

This was spurred on by the Second Vatican Council, known commonly as Vatican 2, held over several years during the early to mid-1960s. Among the topics covered was a historic decision to authorize and promote Bible reading by all Roman Catholics in their heart language. Up to this point, Catholic masses were performed in Latin, and Catholics outside the priesthood were strongly discouraged and in some countries even forbidden to read the Bible in their own language. Traditional priests routinely collected and publicly burned Bibles before Vatican 2. In contrast, a nickname for evangelicals in Latin America at this time was "people of the Book" as Catholics knew evangelicals read and studied the Bible for themselves.

This Vatican 2 edict promoting Bible reading and teaching catapulted the evangelical church in Latin America from being despised and rejected to being highly respected. Catholics were now flooding into evangelical bookstores to buy Bibles and other Christian books. In February 1971, a Catholic priest invited Bill and me to sell the Spanish version of *Good News New Testament*, a modern language translation popular across many denominations, in the cathedral's vestibule after mass. He encouraged every family in his parish to purchase a copy.

Such invitations became widespread. Countless Costa Rican families began reading God's Word. Tent and outdoor campaigns, conversions, miracles, and answers to prayer grew throughout the country. Similar scenes could be found all across Latin America. In fact, the explosion of evangelical churches in Latin America can be attributed in large part to this historic Roman Catholic church decision. Over the following decades, the percentage of evangelicals across Latin America climbed from less than two percent of the population to ten percent to twenty and in some countries now over thirty percent of the population.

During our third semester of language school, Bill and I were expected to begin teaching in the Assemblies of God Bible Institute in San Jose. We were still struggling to speak Spanish, and students often struggled to understand us. But providing new pastors with a solid biblical foundation was why God had called us to Costa Rica, so with much trepidation, we did our best, reminding ourselves of God's promise to the apostle Paul in his own experience of weakness: "My power is made perfect in weakness" (2 Corinthians 12: 9).

One day when teaching a lesson on Jesus's healing of the paralyzed man in John chapter five, I gave the Spanish translation of Jesus's instruction to the paralytic as "drink your milk and walk (*toma tu leche y camina*)" rather than "take up your cot and walk (*toma tu lecho y camina*)." The Spanish word for milk is *leche* while the word for cot is *lecho*, just one letter different, while *toma* can mean to drink or to take/pick up depending on context. I didn't catch my mistake until I saw a puzzled expression on the students' faces and heard their subdued laughs.

The students kindly corrected me, and we laughed together. But they didn't forget my mistake. At the Bible Institute graduation banquet, one of my students who was an artist displayed a drawing he'd done of Jesus giving the crippled man a baby bottle of milk. Under was the caption "Drink your milk and walk!"

Years later when Bill and I visited Costa Rica, these same students, some of them now pastors of mega-congregations, would jokingly greet us with the same expression—drink your milk and walk!

Chapter Eighteen

Students Become Teachers

Students often became my teacher as they shared their stories with me. I learned cultural and spiritual lessons from them that taught me to understand no one and nothing is outside the reach of God's mercy. Our heavenly Father is mercy-full!

During my first year teaching at the Bible Institute, a student named Chico shared his story of how he'd introduced his father's murderer to Christ. When he'd been born more than a month prematurely, his mother was weak and sick, and the banana plantation doctor who'd supervised his birth couldn't save her.

Chico's father had three "wives," one official and two mistresses. One mistress, Florinda, kindly took Chico and his two older sisters into her humble home along with her own three children. Outside of his job delivering goods by mule-back, Chico's dad lived an empty, lonely life composed of drinking, fighting with his machete, and sex. He always won his fights except for his last fatal one.

By the time Chico was seven years old, his "stepmother" Florinda had a new boyfriend named Filemon. The man had been displaying sexual interest in one of Chico's older sisters, which

Chapter Eighteen: Students Become Teachers

infuriated his dad, resulting in a year-long off-and-on war between the two men. One evening Chico's dad showed up at Florinda's home with his mule train. It was getting dark, so while Florinda and Chico tied the mules to a nearby farm fence, Chico's dad lit a kerosene-soaked rag stuffed inside a bottle to give some light.

He was furious when his improvised flashlight showed his enemy Filemon coming towards them. Thrusting the lighted bottle at Florinda, he grabbed his machete and stormed over to Filemon. The other man tried to dissuade him from fighting, but Chico's dad insisted, striking out at Filemon with the machete. Smaller but strong, Filemon threw his opponent to the ground.

Handing seven-year-old Chico the light, Florinda waded into the fray, trying to make peace. It was useless. For the next several minutes, Chico witnessed screams, curses. and gruesome fighting. Recognizing that he was losing, Chico's dad begged forgiveness, but Filemon responded that this was his opportunity to end their ongoing problem.

Despite his dad's bad behavior, Chico loved him. In shock at Filemon's threat, he ran forward, thrusting the burning bottle in his hand against Filemon's bare chest. With a roar of pain, Filemon knocked it away. The bottle crashed to the ground, and the flame went out. They were now in complete darkness.

Crying, Chico stumbled to a neighbor's home, who ran to get the police. Chico could hear his dad's agonizing death screams, then silence. By the time an arriving policeman with a battery-powered lamp lit up the gory scene, Chico's dad had been hacked into pieces. Filemon had even cut off his dad's head before fleeing into the darkness.

The police weren't able to catch Filemon. The next morning, Chico watched with a heavy heart and deep fear as neighbors lowered the pieces of his dad's body into a large hole in the ground. There was no funeral ceremony or prayer.

How sad and empty life is! the young boy thought. *A few miserable years and then under the ground!*

Later, Chico heard that Filemon's conscience had bothered him to the point that he'd confessed the murder to the police and was sentenced to eight years in Costa Rica's San Lucas Island prison. Those were hard years for Chico. He hated his dad's killer. Without his dad's contribution to the family, there was little to eat. Florinda made porridge from bananas and water, but Chico's two older sisters grew thinner and weaker until they both died from malnutrition.

With his mother, father, and two sisters gone, Chico's one obsession was to kill Filemon. He was furious when he received a letter from Filemon asking Chico's help in reducing his prison sentence since his dad had been the one guilty of attacking Filemon first.

Chico was twelve years old when everything changed. During Holy Week, Costa Rican AG pastor Ramon Rojas, our missionary colleague David Kensinger, and Gene Martin, an evangelist visiting from the United States, knocked on Florinda's door and invited the family to an evangelistic outreach. That day at the outreach, Chico heard for the first time that God loved him and had sent His son Jesus to die for him.

Chapter Eighteen: Students Become Teachers

"It's simple," the preacher explained. "If anyone asks Him, Jesus will save them from sin and transform their lives."

Along with forty others that day, Chico accepted Christ and His priceless gift of salvation. He began growing spiritually. The pastor showed him from the Bible that he must forgive even his dad's killer. Gradually, God's love replaced Chico's destructive hate.

One day while Chico was joining a mule train he'd be traveling with, he noticed a familiar-looking man mounting the front of the train. Could that possibly be his father's killer? He took a closer look. It was!

In contrast, Filemon showed no signs of recognizing Chico since he'd grown into a young man during Filemon's imprisonment. As Chico stared at Filemon, hate and vengeance bubbled up inside. Ducking hastily behind a nearby tree, Chico cried out, *God, I can't control these ugly feelings! Please help me now!*

God calmed his spirit with divine strength. Chico mounted the back of the mule train as far from Filemon as he could. For the next two hours, Chico relived the awful tragedy as they travelled together, but with God's strength he no longer felt hate for his dad's murderer.

Chico soon learned that Filemon had moved back into the area and had a shoe repair business he was running out of his home. Each Sunday, Tuesday, Thursday, and Saturday, Chico walked over an hour along a dirt road to get to church. One day Chico realized his route took him right past Filemon's shoe repair business. He prayed for God's help to communicate the good news of the gospel to his father's murderer. Then he opened the shop door.

The odor of leather and glue was strong as Chico introduced himself. Filemon was stunned to learn his identity and avoided eye contact. Chico didn't even mention his dad but just shared the gospel, then left.

Chico returned several times, sometimes with a friend who was one of our Bible Institute students. At first, Filemon thought Chico must have ulterior motives for visiting him, maybe even plotting revenge. But he eventually recognized that Chico was sincere in offering forgiveness and sharing the gospel. He accepted Chico's invitation to church, where God spoke to him powerfully.

Chico joined Filemon at the altar as he accepted Christ as Savior. From that moment, Filemon was transformed from a murderer to a child and saint of God. God had lovingly forgiven him and so had Chico. They embraced each other and cried in God's presence.

Filemon and Chico were now brothers in Christ. Together they sang, prayed, and shared their stories of God's forgiveness. Since they lived in a sparsely populated area, both men were well-known, and many were amazed to see and hear how a murderer and his victim's son could sing God's praises together. Only God could bring such a restoration!

Another student named Manuel also shared his story with us. His dad was an abusive husband and father. When Manuel was nine, his dad left his mother, brother, and Manuel without money, food, or clothing beyond what they wore. His mother and her two sons found a bridge under construction. Scavenging some left-over wood and nails, Manuel and his brother built a little shack in which to live. The family attended the Catholic church, where Manuel served as an altar boy helping the local priest with the mass.

As Manuel grew older, a Christian pastor befriended him, sharing his own vibrant faith. After searching the Scriptures, Manuel accepted Christ. As he grew spiritually, he felt God calling him to serve as a pastor. He knew he needed Bible training, so he applied to the Assemblies of God Bible Institute. He was in his second year of Bible training when Bill and I met him, and his one desire was to spread the good news wherever God led him.

Costa Rican Students.

Chapter Nineteen

Do Angels Wear Overalls?

Communication was challenging in Costa Rica in the 1970s. With no cell phones and few landlines, communications with outlying churches mostly depended on personal messages being passed on through district leaders who met monthly in the capital. Local radio stations also dedicated airtime exclusively to communicate personal messages.

Bill had been assigned to direct a national youth camp in a rural camp site. Several hundred young people were expected. Bill sent messages to three AG church women known for their cooking skills who often helped at such events, requesting their services for the youth camp. But his messages had gone astray, and only one cook arrived.

The open-air kitchen consisted of a large wooden slab table, large metal cooking pots with banana-leaf lids set on stones around a wood-fire, and buckets of water hauled from a nearby river. On the first morning of camp, I introduced myself to the cook in my limited Spanish and asked how I could help.

"Sister Hilda, would you like to cut cabbages for lunch today?" she asked.

"I'll be most happy!" I responded.

"Wonderful! There are the sacks of cabbages and here is a knife. You can cut them on that table." The cooked handed me a razor-sharp knife and indicated three sacks of cabbages.

Lifting a few cabbages to the wooden slab, I went to work, carefully removing the outer leaves, cutting out the hard core, then slicing the cabbage as finely as I could. After an hour, I was on my third cabbage when the cook abruptly spoke up. "Sister Hilda, the cabbages are for salad today!"

She didn't mention that I was being extremely slow and awkward before suggesting kindly, "Could you please ask a couple of young ladies from the morning Bible study session to help?"

The girls graciously accepted my invitation. I watched as they washed each cabbage in a bucket, then artistically used sharp knives like a speedy machine to finely cut the entire cabbage. I was amazed and embarrassed at how quickly they'd accomplished the task. Clearly, I had much to learn about cooking in this rustic setting.

Feeling useless, I spoke up timidly. "Is there something else I could do?"

"Yes, of course. Here is a sack of chayotes that needs peeling." The cook indicated a sack of pear-shaped, green squash-type vegetables.

The girls helped me carry the sack to the riverbank, where we found a flat stone on which to work. With my razor-sharp knife, I began peeling the spiky, fuzzy skin. Sticky moisture from the chayote's flesh stuck to my hands like rubber gloves so I had to keep stopping to wash my hands in the river.

Hours later, my mission was finally accomplished. I carried the peeled chayotes back to the cook, who graciously thanked me. But for the rest of camp week, I volunteered instead to set tables, wash dishes, and serve up the delicious meals our camp cook and her team prepared. That at least was within my capabilities!

Bill enjoyed directing and teaching campers. But a new adventure awaited him when he offered to purchase the chickens for *arroz con pollo* (yellow rice with shredded chicken), a traditional Costa Rican feast that was typically the highlight of camp meals.

"Where do I buy chickens?" he asked the Costa Rican camp staff.

"Any house where you see chickens," he was told. "You'll need to purchase twenty."

Bill took along one of the teen campers to help. Parking the truck he was driving, which belonged to one of the missionaries, at the first farmhouse with a flock of chickens, he asked the farmer if he could purchase twenty.

"Yes, of course," the farmer agreed. "Just catch the ones you want and put them in your sacks."

Bill paid the agreed amount. Then he and his teen helper waded into the flock of chickens. There was much laughter as the farmer and his family watched this tall North American city novice trying to grab chickens. With the farmer's help, twenty chickens were finally caught, bound by the feet, and stuffed into sacks. The sacks jumped around the truck bed as Bill hauled them to the camp kitchen. Thankfully, I wasn't asked to help kill, pluck, and clean them. But I did enjoy the delicious feast of chicken and yellow rice.

Despite many inconveniences, youth camp was a significant milestone of spiritual progress for the young people attending. Boys slept on hard wooden benches in the open-air tabernacle while girls crammed in rustic dormitory bunkbeds. Their testimonies of God working in their lives was our reward. Many responded to the gospel invitation given in each session, and several committed to invest their lives in full-time service to God. Late into the night, we would hear young voices praising God in Spanish and in heavenly languages.

When camp ended, we were tired but happy. We had acquired a small British Sunbeam car for our personal vehicle, and it was tightly packed as we headed home. Our youngest, Cheryl, sat in the space between the bucket-style front seats Bill and I were occupying. Phil and Ruth shared the back seat with a Bible School student named Fonseco.

We were driving along an extremely curvy mountainous road when our car suddenly began making strange noises, then started to jerk. Bill managed to pull over to the side of the narrow road. While the rest of us offered moral support, he tinkered with the engine, trying to determine the problem. But he had no success, and the sun was setting. We were far from help with no accessible garage, telephone, or even a house in sight, and we would soon also be in total darkness.

We considered options. Should we walk toward San Jose, still many miles ahead? Someone would need to remain behind to protect the car and camping gear from potential thieves. If we all stayed, it would likely be daybreak before any motorist came by to flag down. Our British car was unique enough that we knew of only one garage in San Jose with the necessary tools for that make and model. So it wasn't likely any mechanic we could find close-by could repair it. What should we do?

Our Bible school student Fonseco was watching our despondent faces. He finally spoke up. "Brother Bill, have you done everything you can?"

"Yes," Bill responded sadly. "I just don't have an answer!"

"Can we pray?" Fonseco asked.

In truth, the rest of us didn't feel like praying. But we agreed, holding hands in a huddle as Fonseco began to pray. After asking God to provide an answer to our vehicle problem, he concluded with a hearty "Amen! Thank you, Jesus!"

Just then, we saw an elderly jeep coming toward us on that empty road. Spotting our car stopped at the side of the road, the driver slowed down, then stopped. Two men dressed in mechanic's overalls jumped out. Walking over, they immediately put their heads together under the hood and examined the engine.

Amazingly, they seemed to know at once the cause of our trouble. Reaching into their large overall pockets, they pulled out the precise foreign tools and needed part for our British model of car. Working silently, they had the engine repaired within a few minutes. Bill turned the key. The car started immediately. We offered the two mechanics payment for their valued assistance. They wouldn't accept a penny.

"It has been a pleasure to serve you," they stated simply. Climbing back into their elderly jeep, the two men made a U-turn in the road and headed back in the direction from which they'd come.

We were left too astounded for words. Who had told these two men we had car trouble? How did they know at a glance exactly what the problem was? Why would they have been carrying in their large overall pockets the unique tools needed for our British vehicle? Much less the exact needed part? And if they'd been heading somewhere along this road when they came upon us, why had they immediately returned in the direction from which they'd come?

We couldn't answer. What we do know is that these two mechanics were messengers sent from God in response to Fonseco's childlike trust expressed in simple prayer. God miraculously helped a tired, frustrated missionary family stranded on an isolated road far from human help.

Turning to my husband, I asked, "Honey, do angels wear overalls?"

Chapter Twenty

How Long is Your Skirt?

Along with other ministry, we attended as a family an Assemblies of God church in San Jose. One Sunday morning, I had just exited from the service with two-year-old Cheryl in my arms when one of the female ministry leaders attending that church stopped us.

"How long is her skirt?" she asked, indicating my daughter.

That was not a question I was prepared to answer, though certainly to my mind Cheryl's skirt adequately covered her chubby legs and frilly panties. With a flow of fast, melodic Spanish that I struggled to follow, the woman proceeded to use her extended hand to measure the skirt. This was actually a norm for Costa Rican seamstresses, who used hand and arm measurements for fitting and cutting material rather than a tape measure.

She quickly made her measurements and left. I went on home with a heavy heart as my assumption from what I'd caught of her swift Spanish was that she was criticizing Cheryl's cute skirt as being too short for proper church attire. In the seventies, many of the Latin American pastors practiced and preached such legalism.

But exactly how was a two-year-old's too-brief skirt supposed to be some kind of sinful temptation?

I soon realized I needed to deal with my own judgmental heart. One of my ministry responsibilities was helping direct the national AG girls discipleship program called Missionettes. The woman who had accosted us was a leader in this ministry, and I had to work closely with her. Each time I prayed for her, my mind saw her measuring Cheryl's skirt with her hands. I allowed this to become an invisible but very real wall between us.

About two months later, I was once again leaving the Sunday morning service when this same woman edged her way over to me. She offered me an artistically wrapped box. Surprised, I asked, "What is this? It's not my birthday!"

"Open it! Open it!" she insisted.

When I opened the box, I was astonished what I saw. It was a little girl's skirt made of beautiful royal-blue taffeta and hand-painted with orchids and the colorful oxcarts that have become a symbol of Costa Rica. Tears flowed as I remembered my incorrect assumption when this woman had measured Cheryl. She hadn't been criticizing my daughter's skirt length but measuring her to create this beautiful painted work of art.

Kneeling later by my bedside, I asked God to forgive me for having jumped to such a judgmental conclusion. I asked Him to help me accept people as they are and leave the judging to the only true Judge who sees motives as well as actions. This woman and I became good friends and colleagues.

Chapter Twenty: How Long is Your Skirt?

During this time period, my dad had been struggling with Mother's death. He wrote Bill and me how he found himself crying uncontrollably during sleepless nights as he reflected on God's call to India and his deep grief over Mother dying there. His doctor had suggested three options. Either Dad should return to the United States to live with his daughters, marry, or take prescribed medication to sleep.

We were very happy when Dad shared that he'd met a lovely much younger Christian Indian woman named Christine who worked in a Bangalore furniture store. One day while in the store, Dad noticed a New Testament on her desk and invited her to an evangelistic service in a local church. That Sunday, Christine visited the church, where she heard a powerful message from God's Word. She'd known about the Christian God from attending the Church of England as a child and later studying in a Christian boarding school. But she'd never personally experienced Him. That day Christine went forward at the altar call and committed her life and service to Jesus.

Not long after this, Dad and Christine were married. We were delighted when Dad and Christine had a son they named David. We teasingly called Dad "Father Abraham" since he was much older than Christine. After three daughters, he was now the proud father of a beautiful son.

Years later when David was twelve, my two sisters and I traveled to India to visit Dad and his new family. We enjoyed every moment together. Our little brother was very intelligent and rode his bicycle each day to attend a Christian private school. Christine prepared delicious meals for us. Dad and Christine blessed and served each other and countless others for over twenty-three years before Dad passed away.

In 1972, I accepted the opportunity to start a mail-delivered outreach called the International Correspondence Institute. Through newspaper advertisements, hundreds requested the first Bible lesson titled "The Great Questions of Life," then further discipleship lessons. This powerful literature reached professional offices, mountain villages, banana farms, coffee plantations, city workers, college students, nuns and priests, and housewives. Over thirteen thousand people had soon studied God's Word through ICI, and many shared their new-found faith.

In the early 1970s, we saw revival everywhere we went. One time Bill preached two morning services in a church just four years old that already had over sixteen hundred in attendance. Our International Correspondence Institute secretary Lizbeth felt burdened to see a Spirit-filled witness in the Costa Rican town of Aserri. She and her brother found a house to rent on the main road, then asked the landlord's permission to pull down the living-room wall to make more meeting space. We printed invitations on our mimeograph machine, and they went from house to house inviting people to the opening of a new spiritual lighthouse. Within two years, the congregation had grown to two hundred and was supporting a full-time pastor.

In April 1974, a new church was planted in Desamparados, a suburb of the capital. American missionary evangelists Rev. and Mrs. Richard Jeffrey held outdoor services. Many accepted Christ nightly. God healed a malignant tumor, later confirmed by X-rays, one of many such miracles.

With all these wonderful workings of God's Spirit, we encountered many challenges and adventures as well. It was during this time period that my dear husband Bill survived the train derailment that badly injured his back, as I shared in the first chapter of this book. That was only one of countless travel dangers we experienced over the years in Costa Rica.

On another occasion, Bill was driving a Chevy pickup with over three hundred thousand miles on the vehicle while field director William Brooke drove an elderly red van on an extended trip to teach Bible seminars in a remote banana zone. The vehicles also gave the men a place to sleep. During the trip, the two vehicles had to cross a long railway bridge a banana company had built across a wide, deep river. Two-by-twelve planks had been laid alongside the railroad ties so that pedestrians could cross—and the occasional vehicle.

Bill and William had no choice but to drive across if they were to reach their next teaching location. Their major concern was keeping their tires on the planks to avoid from getting cut by or caught in between the train track rails. And, of course, to get across and off the bridge before a train came. It was nerve-racking but God protected them, and they made it across safely.

Another time we were travelling in our small Sunbeam car with our three children sitting snugly in the back seat. The winding dirt road demanded careful driving. Without air conditioning, we kept the windows wide open.

Suddenly, a large truck sped past our little car, showering us with stones and dirt. A large stone whizzed like a bullet through Bill's open window, passed in between the children's heads, then shattered the back windshield. Stopping to investigate, we realized how miraculously God had spared my husband and children from what could have been serious harm. Together we thanked God for His divine protection.

We often had to ford streams where there were no bridges. One of us would walk into the water barefooted to test the depth. If it was too deep to cross, we placed large stones in the creek bed over which our car could bounce to the other side.

A motorized barge ferried passengers and several cars at a time across one wide, fast-flowing river along which there were many towns and villages. We had boarded the barge in our vehicle and were halfway across when the barge motor stopped. Immediately, the barge began drifting with the current. Being the tallest of the passengers, my husband jumped off into the water. Thankfully, it was shallow enough for him to stand up. Tugging on a rope, he gradually pulled the entire barge to the riverbank.

We expressed our feelings in a ministry newsletter we wrote shortly before the end of our first term of service in Costa Rica in 1975.

We feel joy and fulfilment at the end of our first four-year term of service. God sent two hundred and fifty students to the Bible School this year. A record! It was challenging with little sleep, counseling, and learning how to make challenges into strengths and character to be better teachers.

We received many responses like the following from our faithful prayer and financial supporters back in the United States.

We pray that strength and endurance will be your portion . . . patience and firmness when needed . . . may each chapel service be visited from heaven . . . let each class be led by the Holy Spirit . . . we pray for Bill and Hilda . . . provide all their needs.

God answered their prayers beyond all our dreams. He sent great teachers and co-workers. He worked in and through the students and us as well.

Chapter Twenty-One

An Evil Day

We needed those prayers and came to feel the love of God's people in a special way on one occasion in particular as we encountered a very different kind of danger along the road. On December 23, 1972, a devastating earthquake in neighboring Nicaragua killed thousands. In the capital city of Managua, two-thirds of the population was displaced, facing food shortage and disease. Bill had driven a truck loaded with emergency supplies intended for relief efforts there, but Nicaraguan officials confiscated its contents at the border, promising they would distribute the goods to the needy. We learned later that most of this aid went directly to the army.

Not long after the earthquake, we joined a number of other missionary colleagues in a caravan of several vehicles to drive from Costa Rica to Guatemala for the bi-annual Central American Assemblies of God missionary retreat taking place at a rural retreat center in Guatemala's majestic mountains. Our Suburban held two couples with six children between us, the other couple brand-new missionaries still in language school.

Chapter Twenty-One: An Evil Day

The route followed the Pan-American Highway, which took us right through the center of Managua. As we approached the Nicaraguan capital, the smell and sights were horrifying. We gasped at crumbled buildings piled over human remains. One such mountain of rubble had been a nun's convent housing more than two hundred nuns. Our daughter Ruth recalls seeing dogs hauling off human body parts in their mouths.

In the apostle Paul's powerful discussion of spiritual warfare and the armor of God (Ephesians 6:10-20), Paul tells us why it is so vital that we put on God's armor in its entirety "that you may be able to withstand in the evil day, and having done all, to stand firm" (Ephesians 6:13, ESV). Our caravan was returning from a wonderful retreat, spiritually and physically, with our missionary colleagues from all over Central America when we experienced what can be described as just such an *evil day*. Our daughter Ruth described this day in a college English assignment as "My Worst Day."

From Guatemala, we'd passed through El Salvador and Honduras, then entered Nicaragua. Our vehicle was the last of the missionary caravan. The men of our two families shared the driving. We were approaching the town of Chinandega about forty miles into Nicaragua when a pickup truck heading the opposite direction abruptly pulled over to the side of the highway.

The truck was functioning as an illegal public transport, the rear bed dangerously overflowing with passengers. As our vehicle approached, a teenaged boy jumped from the truck bed and dashed across the highway without looking for oncoming traffic. Our colleague was driving at the time and instantly slammed on the brakes.

But it was too late to avoid hitting the young man. The impact hurled him across the road. We immediately stopped our vehicle, and the two men climbed out to check on the young man. He had no pulse.

The impact had dented our vehicle, but it was still drivable. Other passengers were already piling out of the pickup bed to investigate the accident. Unlike North America or the UK, there was no highway patrol to call or anything we could do by staying. In fact, we were well aware of the potential danger as a group of obviously foreign adults and children if the passengers chose to turn on us, a likely scenario regardless of whether the accident had been our fault.

So though heartbroken, we drove on into Chinandega, praying for God's protection and guidance. We found a gas station where another vehicle from our convoy had stopped to gas up, waiting impatiently for service. Pulling in, we explained to them what had happened. We then drove on to the city's central police station to report the accident. The two men of our party entered the police station while we two wives and our six children remained in the vehicle.

A short time later, the pickup truck packed with passengers pulled up close to us. We quickly rolled up the windows. The passengers all jumped out of the pickup truck, surrounding our car in an angry mob. They violently rocked the vehicle, trying to overturn it. They screamed curses and threatened to tear our children limb from limb because we'd killed one of them. Holding each other close, we all prayed fervently.

Chapter Twenty-One: An Evil Day

Thankfully, a group of armed soldiers emerged from the police station and dispersed the crowd. After what seemed an eternity, two police officers escorted our husbands to our vehicle. They explained that our vehicle would be confiscated. Wives and children could proceed on their journey, but the two men would be held in custody while the accident was investigated by specialists.

Our new missionary colleague who had been driving was in shock, unable to muster up the Spanish he'd been learning in language school. Bill took charge of translating and working out legal transactions. The Nicaraguan authorities agreed that the two men could stay in a nearby hotel at night, but police escorts would accompany them to the jail each day.

By this time, the other convoy vehicle that had stopped to gas up arrived at the police station. They offered to cram the two wives and six children into their vehicle, squeezing our luggage in a hitched trailer they were towing. Though they had a large car, it was now packed with children sitting on all available laps.

We all prayed together. Then the other missionary wife and I kissed our husbands goodbye, and we drove away with crushed hearts. Would our husbands be safe? Would they be treated justly? We had no idea when we'd see them again or if the confiscated vehicle would be returned.

As we drove along, one of the children looked behind and noticed that the top to the now overstuffed trailer had popped open and its contents were flying out. Stopping to investigate, we discovered that it was our family's possessions which had been lost, including clothing, accessories, Bibles, and notes from the retreat. It would be pointless to turn around to look for our treasures, since they'd have been snatched up immediately. So we just forced the trailer top back into place and continued.

It was late afternoon when we arrived in Managua. We found a restaurant where our car would be in view, but when we returned to our vehicle after a quick meal, we discovered that someone had slit our tires. Another delay followed as we located a nearby mechanic who painstakingly repaired the slit tires. We then took our accompanying mother and three children to stay with colleagues serving in Managua.

At last our remaining convoy arrived at the Costa Rican border. We were so happy to be this close to home, but joy turned to concern when one of the missionaries couldn't find her passport. We prayed together once again for God's intervention. The immigration agents eventually allowed us all to enter our adopted home country. Crossing the border, we thanked God for His provision and protection but also prayed for our men in Nicaragua.

We'd had no communication with them so didn't know the challenges they were facing. Those of us now safely in Costa Rica later learned the details. Their hotel room was not secure, so they'd had to place a dresser against the door for protection, and due to a drought, there was no water for bathing. The local judge assigned to the case immediately showed himself corrupt, proposing to wine and dine our two men, including an offer of his household maids for their sexual pleasure. Our husbands were horrified.

Meanwhile, the investigators checked tire marks on the highway, the impact on the vehicle, and reports from witnesses.

They found that our car had been driven under the speed limit. The truck was being illegally used as public transportation. The young man should have looked for oncoming vehicles. Bill and his colleague were absolved of guilt.

But despite this, the judge demanded an enormous amount of money, explaining that he had to cover the expenses of the investigation and reimburse the victim's family since the young man contributed to the family budget. Bill refused this proposal, stating that he would personally meet with the victim's father and provide him finances to cover funeral expenses as well as his son's wages for a few months.

The father turned out to be a Christian and an honest, kindly man. As they talked, Bill discovered that this father had lost another son during the recent earthquake, the family's second tragic loss within weeks. The man understood his son was responsible for the accident and didn't want compensation. But Bill insisted. AG headquarters wired the necessary finances from their emergency fund to a missionary serving in Nicaragua, who drove down to Chinandega with the funds. After five long, hot days of negotiations with the unjust judge, our men were released, and our damaged vehicle was returned to them.

They drove immediately down to cross the border into Costa Rica, where they were finally reunited with their families. A nasty red rash covered Bill's body, which a doctor diagnosed as a reaction to the trauma, excessive heat, and lack of water for bathing.

We didn't know that our home church in San Jose under Pastor Enrique Vargas's leadership had heard about the accident.

He'd immediately arranged an all-night prayer meeting. Gathering together, the church members prayed, "God, if you used Paul and Silas in prison, then use your servants in this Nicaraguan jail."

When we arrived to worship the following Sunday morning, it felt like a happy family reunion. Our Spanish was still very limited, and our relationships with these Costa Rican brothers and sister in Christ were still very new. Yet they had sacrificed their Friday night and Saturday morning to pray for God's protection for our family. As we arrived, they hugged, and together we shed tears of joy. That was the moment we knew we were truly loved, accepted, and appreciated by our precious Costa Rican church family.

Chapter Twenty-Two

Reverse Culture Shock

We returned to the United States in 1975 for our first one-year missionary furlough. I was surprised to find myself constantly shocked and angry. I cried through our first English church service in Miami, Florida. The pews were padded. Everyone had a hymn book and Bible. The air-conditioned temperature was ideal. Yet the worship seemed rote like a faucet turned on and off.

This isn't fair! I remember telling myself. The previous Sunday I'd been sitting on a wooden plank while my husband preached under a mango tree, the only shade from Costa Rica's burning sun. Yet our Costa Rican believers sang vibrantly and responded visibly to God's Word.

Later when visiting a local mall, we saw people carrying large bags of purchases. Towels and bedding came in a myriad of colors. Dress racks seemed never-ending with styles to please anyone. Such an abundance raised questions. When these people had so much, why wasn't I seeing smiles and happy faces?

I eventually learned that I was suffering from what is termed reverse culture shock. Just as I'd been shocked at all the changes and poverty and new experiences when we arrived in Costa Rica, so I was now shocked at all the wealth, conveniences, and extravagance Americans enjoyed in comparison with other developing-world countries.

As I confessed my negative feelings to God, it seemed that He whispered to me: "Hilda, you're not seeing the big picture. Many in this culture express their worship and commitment more reservedly, but they still love me. And many are channels through which I bless others."

God taught me to follow His example to accept and love people as they are regardless of where we were living. During that furlough, we again stayed, studied, and worked at the Overseas Ministries Study Center in Ventnor, NJ. One summer afternoon during our stay, our son Phil, now eleven years old, was playing in the courtyard when an elderly gentleman approached him to say that he was a medical missionary serving in India and was looking for housing at the Center while attending a medical convention in nearby Atlantic City.

Knowing my own heart for India, Phil ran into our apartment to ask me if the Center had an available room for the gentleman. I checked, but as usual during summer months, all apartments and guest rooms were filled. Walking outside with Phil to meet the stranger, I told him, "Sorry, sir, but there is nothing available."

"Mom, he can stay in my room!" Phil interrupted. "I'll change the sheets!"

I was frustrated by Phil's offer. I'd just returned with my children the night before from a busy weekend of ministry in New York City, and my husband was still on the road visiting supporting

Chapter Twenty-Two: Reverse Culture Shock

churches. I didn't know this gentleman and certainly wouldn't invite any man into our home without my husband present. Nor had I shopped for groceries or cleaned our house for guests.

Introducing himself as Dr. Rambo, the stranger explained that he'd already checked local hotels, but the cheapest cost was twenty-five dollars a night, equivalent today of over a hundred-twenty-five dollars a night. The money spent on a hotel room for a week could help a lot of patients in India, so he'd come to the Center, assuming that as a missionary he could qualify for a guestroom.

Reluctantly, I invited Dr. Rambo onto our verandah while Phil and I cleaned my son's bedroom. Then Phil brought the doctor and his suitcase into his room. Dr. Rambo immediately knelt and thanked God for opening the heart of this boy and giving him such a lovely place to stay. As I witnessed this, I was humiliated and ashamed since God knew that my own heart wasn't open. I served Dr. Rambo a simple meal of bacon and eggs, the only groceries I still had in the refrigerator. His voice cracked with emotion as he thanked God for this delicious meal.

We soon learned that Dr. Rambo was an eye surgeon and at eighty years old had been removing cataracts and restoring sight to countless thousands of poor Indians for decades. I was delighted when Bill returned home while Dr. Rambo was there. They became good friends, and Bill offered him transport to his medical convention.

One morning while arriving at the convention, Dr. Rambo asked Bill to stop the car. He'd spotted two medical delegates dressed in Indian clothing. Bill pulled over, and Dr. Rambo got out to introduce himself to the two Indian doctors. Bill listened as Dr. Rambo reminded the two men that their country desperately needed them and encouraged them to return to serve to India's poor with needed medical equipment.

Dr. Rambo and Phil exercised early each morning on the boardwalk. One morning while Bill and I were having devotions on the front porch, Dr. Rambo returned with Phil. He looked very distressed with a flushed face and purple lips.

"What's the matter, Dr. Rambo?" Bill and I asked him.

"You believe in God's power to heal, right?" he asked. "Please pray with me for my heart. Then I will go lie down. If I can rest a bit, I should be fine."

We prayed urgently, asking God to touch His dear servant. Then Dr. Rambo went into his room to rest. Thankfully, he was looking much better when he got up. Dr. Rambo went to a local clinic, and they immediately took an EKG. The exam showed that he'd suffered a heart attack but his heart was presently ticking well. Together we thanked God.

When the convention was over, we were reluctant to say goodbye. Later as we read the literature Dr. Rambo had left with us, we realized he was world-famous. He'd received a gold **medal from King George VI** in 1941 for exceptional public service. In 1957, he'd been elected president of India's ophthalmological society. He'd also been recognized for his service as director of a major Christian hospital by India's prime minister **Indira Gandhi**. In 2008, Dr. Rambo was posthumously inducted into the Medical Missions Hall of Fame.

Chapter Twenty-Two: Reverse Culture Shock

Dr. Rambo's visit ended up becoming the highlight of my furlough. He was a unique blessing I'd nearly missed, but thanks to Phil's open, loving heart, I felt we'd entertained an angel unaware!

Later during that furlough year, I went to a nearby beauty salon for a hair trim. I'd never met this particular beautician. As we conversed about life's most important values, she began opening up her heart's secrets with me. The more we talked, the more she cut. When she finally finished, she turned the chair around so I could look in the mirror.

My heart immediately sank. My hair had been cut so short I could have been mistaken for a man. I paid the bill and left, thanking God that at least I'd been able to share His good news with a searching young woman. But I knew how disappointed Bill would be as he liked shoulder-length hair on me. I didn't want to go home with that haircut, so I started walking slowly along the boardwalk. Maybe I was figuring the sea breeze would grow my hair!

Finally, I headed home. When I opened our front door, Bill was there. Neither of us said a word as he took in my changed appearance. Then he walked over and tightly embraced me.

"Honey, I love you!" he said tenderly. No conditions, no explanation needed. Though I'd heard those precious words many times before, this time was extra special. What a man!

Chapter Twenty-Three

Leave Within Ten Days!

In 1976, we returned to Costa Rica for another four-year term. Finding a three-bedroom house, we signed a four-year rental contract. Minimal sunlight entered the small windows. To brighten our home, I painted the kitchen with yellow daisies, the bathroom with fish, and our girls' room with a flower garden behind a picket fence. Bill made valances for the windows, and I sewed lined draperies, which also served as blinds for privacy. Soon our house was clean and comfortable.

Bill built a skateboard ramp in the driveway for our kids and their friends. Our house quickly became the neighborhood children's hang-out. Neighboring women also joined me for an exercise class in our car port. We held weekly home Bible studies where many neighbors accepted Christ and received the Spirit's infilling. Our oldest daughter Ruth, now fourteen years old, held a Bible story hour for the children in the girls' bedroom while I shared with their mothers in the living room.

One day a neighbor showed up at the exercise class distressed and crying. She shared that thieves had stolen her husband's delivery truck. For security, he'd parked the truck right outside their open bedroom window. But the thieves had sprayed some kind of sedative through the window to render the couple unconscious, a sadly common criminal tactic in Costa Rica. The loss of the delivery truck left the family without an income.

Joining hands and hearts right there in the carport, we all prayed together for divine intervention. After our exercise time, the woman returned home. She'd recently accepted Christ and had started reading a Spanish Bible we'd given her. Randomly opening the Bible, she began reading the account in 2 Kings chapter six where the prophet Elisha miraculously causes an iron axe head that had fallen in a river to float to the surface.

God, if You knew where the axe head was, she prayed, *then You know where our truck is. Will You please help us find it?*

For the next two weeks, we continued to pray for a miracle every time she came to exercise. Her husband had filed a police report, but locating a stolen vehicle in Costa Rica in the 1970s was like finding a needle in a haystack. Then one day the San Jose police station called this couple to report that they'd just raided a garage close to the airport where they'd discovered many stolen vehicles. Perhaps one of those vehicles belonged to them.

Excitedly, our neighbors arrived at the garage, but none of the impounded vehicles resembled their truck. The police advised them to check the actual engine numbers. They quickly found an engine with the same number as their truck. The thieves had painted the truck another color, added stripes, replaced old tires with new mega-sized ones, overhauled the engine, and covered the truck bed with a camper shell. It was indeed their stolen truck, but it now looked, felt, and rode like a new vehicle!

After they'd driven the truck home, this neighbor woman couldn't wait for the next exercise class to share the good news. She visited each of us individually to let us know that God hadn't only rescued the axe head in Elisha's day but had rescued and renovated their stolen truck!

We were very happy and settled as a family in our new home and neighborhood. Then late one night, the doorbell rang. Outside stood our landlady and several extended family members. She announced, "We will be moving in here now. You must leave the house within ten days."

"You have a legal right to stay," our neighbors advised. "You have a four-year contact, so she can't just break the contract when you've lived here for such a short while. We'll help you fight!"

But we decided to leave peacefully. We also left the house sparkling clean. We later learned that our landlady had experienced a painful divorce, which was why she had to move into this rental property. We looked for a similar house to rent, but the only one we could find was bigger and more luxurious. This concerned us as we didn't want to be living in a house that was so fancy our Costa Rican ministry colleagues, believers, and former neighbors would feel uncomfortable. But since we could find no alternative, we rented the bigger house.

Thankfully, our Costa Rican friends and neighbors didn't respond negatively at all. Instead, they assured us, "We know why you had to leave this neighborhood. God had a nicer house for you!"

Eight years later when we returned to Costa Rica for another term, we found a rental just a few blocks from our former

Chapter Twenty-Three: Leave Within Ten Days!

flower/fish-painted house. That Christmas, I knocked on each door along our street to invite the women to a Christmas fiesta in our home. I had no idea how many would come, but thirty-five eventually squeezed into our living room, filling every chair and sitting on the floor.

We sang Christmas carols around the piano, ate goodies I'd prepared, shared examples of how God had intervened in our lives, and prayed together. As gifts, I presented each with festively wrapped Scripture posters. I also offered to hold exercise classes and/or Bible studies in their homes.

Several women stayed behind to ask for individual prayer. One of these invited Bill and me to start a Bible study in her home. Only when she introduced herself did we realize she was our former landlady who'd ordered us out of her house eight years earlier. She'd accompanied one of my new neighbors who'd received my invitation to the Christmas fiesta.

How exciting it was for Bill and me to be welcomed into our former living room, where we found several couples hungry to hear God's Word. It had been hard to leave the home into which we'd put so much hard work and love. But now we were reaping spiritual fruit from seeds sown eight years earlier by leaving our former rented house sparkling clean and with a positive attitude. God had literally re-opened an abruptly closed door to share His amazing love with both new and former neighbors.

That same year in 1983, I was invited to minister in AG women's conferences and Women's Aglow gatherings in the small Central American country of Belize. While there, I was privileged to visit our first AG missionary family commissioned to Belize and fully supported by the national church in Costa Rica. They pastored a vibrant, growing Spanish-speaking congregation and Bible Institute in Orange Walk, Belize.

What a wonderful day to witness missions come full circle from North American missionaries bringing the gospel to Costa Rica to Costa Rican missionaries now carrying the gospel to other nations.

Chapter Twenty-Four

Humpty Dumpty

Smash! A myriad of odd-shaped shards and splinters of ceramic-like shell lay tragically on the tiled floor—the remains of a large ostrich egg I'd dubbed Humpty Dumpty.

Humpty Dumpty had been a gift from Jerry and Lydia Olshevski, AG missionaries serving in Botswana, Africa, who had furloughed at the Overseas Ministries Study Center at the same time our family was there. Carefully wrapping the egg and sealing it in a plastic container, I'd managed to transport it unbroken to Costa Rica, where I'd proudly displayed it on a brass stand in our dining room hutch.

Humpty Dumpty had also become my faithful traveling companion over bumpy, pot-holed roads to women's conferences and events, where the giant egg sat in a brass bowl next to a hen's egg, a visual that allowed me to contrast the maternal care of a hen and an ostrich, then apply biblical principles of child raising. The Costa Ricans would pat Humpty Dumpty in awe as few had seen an egg that big.

Now my heart sank to see Humpty Dumpty strewn over the dining room floor. How could I ever replace her. Sadly, I asked our teenaged son Phil to sweep up the mess and bury her remains in the rubbish can.

Meanwhile, Phil's creative mind clicked into high gear as he looked from my sad face to the floor. A puzzle always challenged him, and he quickly turned the desk in his bedroom into a construction site. With determination and agile fingers, he began rebuilding this white oval puzzle. Day after day and week after week behind his closed bedroom door, he found the original position of each piece, filed the edges with precision, sandpapered, then glued together jagged pieces and splinters.

When he finally finished, Phil gently transferred Humpty Dumpty to his desk drawer. That Christmas Eve, our family gathered in the living room to read the Christmas story. The silver aluminum tree we'd purchased for $6.66 so many years ago was sprinkled with tiny white Styrofoam packing balls, giving the appearance of snow. Under the tree were festively wrapped packages.

After finishing the Scripture reading and praying together, we began opening presents. Phil's gift to me was a large box that weighed so little I wondered if it was a joke with nothing but tropical air inside. When I carefully opened it, I cried with joy. Sitting there in the box was Humpty Dumpty. Thanks to Phil's diligent work of love, she looked beautiful with just a small, jagged hole to remind me she'd been refashioned.

I set her once again on her brass stand in the dining hutch. She has been my Christmas illustration ever since for hundreds of adults and children in many countries, a precious reminder of God's redeeming grace.

Chapter Twenty-Four: Humpty Dumpty

I too was once a fallen Humpty Dumpty, a pile of ugly pieces and splinters without a ray of hope. But God, the Divine Master Craftsman, stooped down to pick up the pieces and remake me into His child reflecting His divine image. God lovingly planned my salvation, sending His beloved Son that first Christmas morning so He could give His life to restore me. While I'm far from perfect with jagged holes, one day I will be complete and without blemish before God.

Thanks, Phil! Thanks, Jesus!

God continued to bless His kingdom and our family in Costa Rica. But we also continued to have adventures that made us deeply grateful for God's protection and intervention. One evening I'd shared God's Word at a new church plant in San Jose. Nine-year-old Cheryl, our youngest daughter, had accompanied me. After the service, I'd spent time in prayer with many new believers, so it was after 10 p.m. when Cheryl and I started home.

We were driving along a dark, empty road when suddenly there was a loud thud as the car's front wheels violently jerked into a huge, unmarked manhole, abruptly stopping us. I tried to drive forward without success. We stopped and prayed together, pleading for God's help. Then I put the vehicle in reverse and stepped on the accelerator. The car instantly bounced back out of the gaping hole, but now it clanged loudly.

"Let's get out and see what's wrong," suggested Cheryl.

"Even if we identify the problem, I can't fix it," I pointed out. "And there's no one around to help."

Instead, we drove on at tortoise speed, clanging loudly all the way home. We finally pulled up safely to our home. When we walked in the front door, the telephone was ringing. Ana, the wife of the new church plant's pastor, was on the line.

"You're home safely, Sister Hilda!" she blurted out with a sigh of relief. "When I said goodbye to you tonight, I was burdened to pray for your safety. As I pushed my baby home in the stroller, I knew you were in danger on the road and needed prayer. I usually prepare something to eat after the evening service, but I was so burdened I just fell on my bed and prayed for you. Thank God you're safe!"

I thanked Ana for obeying God by praying for us. I also thanked God, who'd heard and answered her prayer, for His protection on that dark, empty road.

On another occasion, our children accompanied us during a school vacation to combine evangelistic outreach with family time on Costa Rica's beautiful southern coast. We drove along the two-laned Pan-American highway, mountains towering up to twelve thousand feet above sea level on one side of the road while a river tumbled over boulders down in a valley on the other side. Huge ferns lifted lacy fronds towards the sun, and the verdant jungle foliage spread its shade above the road.

During the tropical rainy season this road could be quite dangerous as water-saturated soil caused frequent landslides, burying highways, cars, homes, and people under masses of rock, uprooted trees, and mud. But that day as we drove along was beautiful with clear blue skies. Zigzagging around the tight curves,

Chapter Twenty-Four: Humpty Dumpty

we turned a sharp, blind corner. Suddenly Bill heard a warning in his spirit as though a voice was shouting, "Stop!!!!"

He slammed on the brakes. Just as we jerked to a halt, a huge boulder at least half the size of our small Sunbeam car crashed down the steep mountainside into the road in front of us, then ricocheted off, continuing down the slope into the angry river. If Bill had braked a second later, it would have crushed our car. Trembling, we realized that God had once again spared our lives. Before driving on down the road, we took time to thank God, our "ever-present help in trouble" (Psalm 46:1 NIV).

Chapter Twenty-Five

Why Speak So Loudly?

Sometime later, Bill and I along with a Costa Rican colleague were scheduled to teach an intensive five-day regional Bible Institute in a town about five hours from San Jose. When we arrived, I waited in line to call our children on that town's only public telephone. A missionary colleague was caring for our children while we were gone.

I finally got through to our house, but the moment I heard our oldest daughter Ruth's voice, I knew something was wrong. "Mom, Cheryl is sick. She and I stayed home from school today, and she is vomiting."

While I was sorry to leave my scheduled students in the lurch, my first responsibility was to our children, so I immediately responded, "I'll catch the next bus to the capital."

Bill and I hurried to the bus terminal, where I was able to get a seat on a bus that would arrive in San Jose about 2 a.m. I'd never travelled long-distance alone on a public bus in Costa Rica. Before I boarded, Bill and I prayed for travelling mercies and that someone kind would sit beside me.

I'd barely settled into my seat when a young man I recognized as an AG Bible Institute student from San Jose climbed onto the bus and sat down next to me. Most of our students were also pastors, and this young man was catching a connecting bus to his home and church. He knew me from the Bible Institute, and we began chatting. Our conversation centered around God's goodness, but he was speaking very loudly.

I'm not deaf! I thought. *Why so loud?*

Then I realized his volume wasn't for my benefit but for the seated and standing passengers who were listening intently to his testimony of God's goodness. While not an evangelistic technique that would work well in North America, it was not uncommon in Costa Rica. The young pastor eventually got to his feet to get off at his stop. As he exited, a woman elbowed her way from the rear of the bus to ask, "May I sit next to you?"

Dropping into the seat the young pastor had vacated, the woman introduced herself as Betty. As the bus headed down the road again, Betty began sharing her past life. She'd drifted away from her Christian faith and went to church merely out of habit. Right there on the bus, God spoke to her. We prayed together, and she recommitted her life to Jesus. I then asked Betty, "Do you live in the town where we caught the bus?"

"No, I just visited there to bring my sister Nelly back to her home and family." Betty went on to explain that her sister had abandoned her husband and four children for a man in that town. Nelly's husband had attended an all-night prayer vigil, where he'd asked God to bring back his wife. The next morning while he'd been plowing his field, his tractor had tipped over, crushing him to death.

"I knew I must tell my sister," Betty went on. "But I didn't have her address, just the town where she lived. When I arrived, I hired a taxi to drive me down each street to look for my sister."

Due to the extreme heat, doors and windows stood open. Miraculously, as the taxi drove slowly down one street, Betty spotted Nelly lying on a bed inside a small shack. When she entered, she could see that her sister was ill.

"What are you doing here, Betty?" Nelly asked. "Last night I dreamed you came for me wearing a blue dress. And here you are dressed in blue."

"I've come because there's a crisis in your family," Betty responded. "You must come back with me right away."

Getting slowly got out of bed, Nelly packed her meager belongings in a paper sack and went with her sister. Betty indicated a plump woman with a sullen expression sitting on the far side of another woman across the aisle from us. "This is Nelly. Sister Hilda, won't you please talk to my sister? She is very hard. She doesn't know her husband has died. She also needs to come back to God."

Turning to the woman sitting next to Nelly, Betty asked if she'd kindly exchange seats with me. The woman was happy to do so since Nelly was quite overweight and hogging most of the two seats. I introduced myself to Nelly, asking a few general questions. She refused to speak. Silently, I asked God for wisdom.

Meanwhile, the bus chauffeur was driving like a crazy man, passing other vehicles at top speed, swerving around large potholes and zig-zag curves despite the uneven dirt road and thick fog.

Passengers were becoming increasingly tense as they clung to bus seats and straps. I finally said to Nelly, "I'm so glad I'm ready for heaven. I'm not sure if we'll arrive at our destination!"

This seemed to get through to Nelly. After a few more moments of hearing the other passengers' angry and fearful complaints, she broke down and began sharing with me. During Holy Week, Nelly had become very ill. Her male partner was deep into witchcraft, but he'd agreed to visit the local Assemblies of God church with her.

Since the church was packed, the couple sat in the last bench. During the message, the pastor hesitated, then spoke words God had given him. "There is someone here tonight who God wants to heal, but you first need to receive His forgiveness."

Nelly knew God was speaking to her. But her male partner, uncomfortable in this sacred atmosphere, grabbed her and dragged her out. The following week, Nelly had dreamed about her sister Betty coming to see her dressed in blue.

"Now here I am," she concluded.

I quickly responded, "Nelly, this is the first time I am travelling alone long distance in a Costa Rican public bus. I didn't plan to be on this bus, but my youngest child is sick in San Jose, so I am going to care for her. Nelly, God spoke to you through the pastor, then in a dream of your sister. Now I am sitting next to you telling you God loves you. He forgives and forgets our past sins. This is the third time God is speaking to you. I don't know if you'll have another opportunity."

As if an internal volcano had erupted, Nelly began crying uncontrollably. Concerned passengers asked if she needed medical help. I explained that she was getting right with God. We prayed together. Finally with a smile, Nelly said, "Sister Hilda, all I have in this world is in the paper bag above me, but I have peace inside. I'm going back to my family and to our local church family."

Despite the chauffeur's erratic driving, the bus arrived safely at the San Jose bus terminal around 2.30 a.m. My son and the missionary colleague caring for our children were there to pick me up. Though still concerned for my sick daughter, I was dancing on the inside.

As we drove home, I shared how divinely planned this "unplanned" bus trip had turned out to be. Two sisters, Betty and Nelly, both travelling away from God, had made a U-turn towards Him. I was ecstatic. I was also now extremely grateful for our Bible Institute student-pastor whose loud conversation had drawn these two women to come and speak to me.

When we arrived home, I found Cheryl curled up on the bathroom floor next to the toilet where she'd been vomiting. As I picked her up and tucked her into bed, I told her softly, "Cheryl, God used you to bring me home on a bus where two ladies recommitted their lives to Jesus. I know God is going to heal you."

Then I prayed over my youngest daughter. When Cheryl got sick, it was typically for at least three days. But as I got up the next morning to get my two older children ready for school, I found Cheryl totally well and able to attend school that day.

Chapter Twenty-Six

Dad Sent Us to Jail

Arenal is a mountainous region of Costa Rica about eighty miles from San Jose best known for its still active Arenal volcano, for Lake Arenal, which is Costa Rica's largest lake, and for its excellent volcanic soil, perfect for growing coffee and macadamia nuts. While Bill and I were ministering in the nearby town of Arenal, a church family named Murillo hosted us on their macadamia nut and coffee plantation. For evening meals, we enjoyed fresh fish speared by the Murillo sons from the Arenal River.

On one visit to their farm, we met the patriarch of the family, who was ninety-three years old and nearly blind. But he still worked a little every day around the farm, and though slow, he always walked the significant distance to church, usually arriving early to spend time in prayer for God's blessing on the service. He always had a smile on his face, and we never heard him complain once.

We could never have guessed the story that lay behind the Murillo patriarch and his family. One of his daughters, Naomi, eventually told us the tale. Back in the 1940s long before Vatican 2, there was still strong opposition to evangelicals. Anyone who broke with the country's dominant national religion to read the

Bible in their own language and worship Jesus without the control and oversight of the Catholic priests were often harshly persecuted.

When Naomi was a young girl, a Costa Rican believer named Elias visited the Murillo family home and shared the good news of Jesus's love and salvation. While Naomi's mother joyfully accepted Jesus into her heart, her dad was strongly opposed. Her mother read a Spanish-language Bible, sang hymns, and prayed with Naomi and her sister Christine each day. But her dad tore up any Christian literature his wife brought into the house and burned her treasured Bible.

A year later, Naomi's mother suddenly died of a heart attack. Her dad assumed that without their mother's influence his two daughters would return to the family's religious tradition. Instead, they continued to follow the biblical teachings of their mother.

In desperation, the dad sent Christine and Naomi to the House of the Good Shepherd, a female jail in San Jose supervised by Roman Catholic nuns. He believed their indoctrination would rescue his daughters from what he thought was an erroneous cult. At eight and nine years old, Christine and Naomi found themselves among murderers, thieves, and prostitutes. The food was unappetizing. They received clean clothes on Sundays, were forced to pick coffee and do household chores, and were unable to attend school.

They were also prohibited from talking except during a brief break time. For every word spoken outside that time slot, they received a demerit. For every demerit, they had to sit in a chair without moving for an hour on Sunday. Although the two sisters suffered in this strange, ungodly atmosphere, they always found time together each day to softly sing the hymns and repeat the Bible texts their mother had taught them. God's love encouraged them.

One day the girls overheard two nuns talking about them. One nun said, "Those girls are so sweet. This is no place for them. They will only learn bad habits from these criminals."

Another added, "Their father said they can only return home if they take First Communion."

First Communion is the Catholic ceremony where Catholic children first participate in taking mass, a major step in being confirmed into the Catholic church, which typically occurs between seven and twelve years old. It involves studying the Catholic catechism as well as going to the confessional to confess their sins to a Catholic priest, whom they've been taught have the power to forgive sin rather than going straight to Jesus in prayer or confession.

Naomi and Christine decided to study for First Communion so they could leave the jail. When they asked a nun about taking First Communion, the nun was delighted. The sisters quickly learned the catechism. But going into the confessional box was harder for them. Pulling back the curtain from the small opening behind which he sat, the priest asked Naomi, "Why are you here, little girl?"

"Because I accepted Jesus as my Savior," Naomi replied.

The priest immediately told her, "Leave that erroneous doctrine from Martin Luther!"

Naomi immediately responded that her trust wasn't in this Martin Luther but in Jesus. She went on to quote one of the Bible verses her mother had taught her: "The gospel is the power of God unto salvation to everyone who believes" (Romans 1:16 NKJV).

With a smile, she told the priest, "You can read that in your Bible."

The following Sunday, Naomi and Christine dressed in pretty white dresses and participated in the sacrament of the Roman Catholic First Communion. In accordance with the arrangement their dad had made with the nuns, the two girls left behind the dreary, lonely female prison, delighted to be home again. Their dad was also happy, thinking that the institutional discipline had erased Jesus from their lives. He was wrong. This hardship only served to strengthen their faith in Jesus.

Christine and Naomi cooked for their older brothers and dad, who worked hard on the farm. The girls enjoyed listening to Christian radio programs, which helped them grow spiritually. But when their dad found out, he sold the radio.

The sisters discovered that one of their uncles was a believer and was holding evangelical meetings in his house. They visited him whenever they could to hear more about Jesus. When their dad realized what was happening, he cut off olive-tree branches and whipped them all the way home until their legs bled.

"Dad, you can kill us if you want," Naomi told him, "but you can never take away what we have in our hearts."

Their dad opted to punish Christine and Naomi another way. He didn't buy any more clothes for them and cut down on food

Chapter Twenty-Six: Dad Sent Us to Jail

purchases, buying enough only for the working men. The girls would eat a little while cooking but frequently went to bed hungry. When they felt especially weak and sick from hunger, they visited the home of a married brother, who fed them.

This older brother finally convinced his dad to let his sisters go to San Jose to work. In God's providence, Naomi found work during the day with a missionary family and went to school at night. She and Christine found an evangelical church to attend, where they sang in the choir and grew spiritually.

Naomi eventually married a fine Christian young man. God blessed the couple with four boys and one girl. Although Naomi's dad wouldn't permit them to talk to him about Jesus, they prayed for him daily.

When Naomi's father was eight-four years old, God gave him a vision of God's outstretched hand and God's voice saying, "Accept me and I will give you this crown of life." But the dad still hardened his heart. God revealed Himself again through the same vision, but he refused to accept. Later, Naomi's dad grew ill, wavering between life and death.

For the third time, the vision appeared to him. This time he recognized that God was speaking. He repented of sin and accepted Jesus as well as His crown of life. He was immediately freed from his prejudice and anger. Within two weeks, he was baptized in water.

The next time Naomi saw her dad, she could barely speak due to tears of joy and thanksgiving to God. For the first time, they were a united family, loving and serving God. Naomi's family invited her dad to live with them on their farm, which is where we met him. After fighting God for so many years, he expressed to us how thankful he was that God's great mercy had saved him. He looked forward to soon seeing Jesus face to face.

Chapter Twenty-Seven

Escape from Death

A former Bible Institute student of ours, Marcelino, had become the pastor of the Assemblies of God church in the town of Arenal. This was actually in a new location since the original town on the banks of the original Lake Arenal had been submerged when a large hydroelectric dam was built, greatly increasing the lake's volume and providing much of Costa Rica's electricity. The government had rebuilt the town on higher ground northeast of the lake, including a new Assemblies of God church to replace the one now underwater.

But while the church now had a new sanctuary, there were no classrooms for Sunday school or discipleship classes to teach children and new believers. Marcelino invited Bill and me to hold a weekend teaching conference on faith at the Arenal church. The culmination of the conference on Sunday evening would include a faith offering to raise funds for building classrooms. Each church family was asked to pledge what they could contribute.

The Sunday evening service was a glorious celebration. Musical groups sang God's praises. Marcelino explained that each family could come forward to the microphone to announce their pledge.

They would then have thirty days to fulfil their promises. Calculator in hand, the church treasurer totaled up the value of each pledge.

Marcelino was first, donating one of his two calves. The family hosting Bill and me pledged a large tree from their farm to provide wooden beams for the construction. The owner of a cinderblock factory pledged materials and equipment to make cinderblocks if church members would provide the labor. Another family promised a pig. A dear grandmother who was an expert at crochet pledged twenty-five hand-made doilies that could be sold for an offering. A little boy who sold newspapers pledged two weeks of his earnings. Others pledged chickens, eggs, tortillas, and empanadas.

Then a poorly-dressed elderly man came shyly to the microphone. He looked nervous and teary-eyed as he shared his sadness that he had nothing to contribute but his labor to help to make cinderblocks. Putting his arm around the man, Bill opened his Bible to Exodus 31 and began reading the names of the craftsmen God had specially anointed to build the tabernacle.

He then turned to the elderly man and explained that God had listed these names in His sacred book because they were important. God had also seen this dear man's tears and valuable offering. In His records, God was adding his name to the list of block-making craftsmen appointed and blessed to build God's house in Arenal.

A huge smile broke out on the elderly man's weathered face as he realized that he was important to God and that God had accepted his gift of labor. The evening closed with a huge applause and praise to the Lord. The goal for construction funds was

Chapter Twenty-Seven: Escape from Death

surpassed as everyone joyfully gave from grateful hearts. Together we had participated in a truly sacred fiesta of giving to our Lord.

Sometime later on a Friday, Marcelino was completing a period of fasting and prayer when he sensed God speaking to him through a specific passage in Psalms.

Our God is a God who saves; from the Sovereign Lord comes escape from death. (Psalm 68:20, NIV)

While Marcelino didn't understand why God had laid this particular verse on his heart, he trusted God. In his journal, he wrote:

God is going to test me in an unusual way, but He lovingly assures me He will be with me and will strengthen me.

That evening, a ministry colleague named Santiago concluded an evangelistic campaign in the Arenal church. The next morning, Santiago headed out on foot to catch a bus back to San Jose while Marcelino loaded Santiago's luggage on the back of his small motorbike, planning to deliver it to Santiago at the bus terminal. As Marcelino was threading his way through the crowded Saturday open air market at the town's central intersection, a speeding Jeep ignored a stop sign and hit Marcelino's motorbike. Marcelino catapulted high into the air, landing hard on the concrete sidewalk.

The crunching metal and squealing rubber drew hundreds of people to the crash site, including some of Marcelino's church members. Stooping over his body, they laid hands on him and prayed, "Dear God, our pastor shouldn't die because of such a terrible accident! Please save his life and heal him for your glory."

For the next few minutes, the farmer's market became a prayer meeting. This included three nuns who assured the gathered church members, "We can't allow this servant of God to die. While you care for him, we will go to the Catholic church and continue praying for him there."

Meanwhile, Marcelino's friends from church carefully lifted his limp, mangled body and carried him to a nearby medical clinic. Dozens followed to see if he was still alive. While Marcelino's helmet had partially protected his head, the clinic doctor determined that he had broken ribs, broken legs, internal hemorrhage, and cerebral trauma.

Emerging to give his status to the concerned bystanders, the doctor stated bluntly, "I can't help him here. You need to take him to the clinic in the city where they have better equipment. Every moment counts, so hurry!"

Semi-conscious, Marcelino heard the doctor's diagnosis and knew he was dying. He labored to breathe as his friends loaded him into a nearby truck and sped over a washboard-rough dirt road to the city two hours away. His legs were paralyzed, and he couldn't move his head. His dislocated collar bone and other broken bones were causing excruciating pain. Thankfully, he soon fell into deep unconsciousness.

When they arrived at the city clinic, the doctor there wouldn't even allow Marcelino's friends to take him out of the truck. Giving

Chapter Twenty-Seven: Escape from Death

him a cursory examination, he confirmed the previous doctor's diagnosis. Marcelino was dying and needed to get to a hospital immediately for emergency surgery to stop internal bleeding.

When they finally reached the emergency room of the closest hospital, Marcelino was carried in to begin a round of X-rays and medical procedures before surgery could be performed. His church friends stayed in the truck, praying for God's mercy and healing. But as the emergency room doctors examined successive X-rays, they grew confused. Marcelino's most recent X-rays looked as though they belonged to a completely different person. They showed no trace of blood accumulation from internal hemorrhaging nor any broken bones. Marcelino could now move his legs.

In a dilemma, the doctors transferred Marcelino to an observation room and took more X-rays and other tests. His condition continued to improve. Late in the day, a specialist came by to explain the test to Marcelino.

"It's unbelievable what has happened to you, Marcelino. When you arrived, you had multiple fractures and internal bleeding. We saw death in your face. We planned to operate immediately to save your life. Then suddenly while we were taking X-rays, your vital signs stabilized, and I saw the spark of life come back into your eyes. We'll observe you for a couple more hours, but you appear to be healed."

Marcelino had no doubt that God had healed him. He was soon discharged and walked unassisted to the truck where the church friends who'd driven him to the hospital were praying.

They praised God together for God's healing of their pastor and friend. Later as Marcelino reread his journal entry from the night before the accident, he realized what God had been saying to him. Like the verse he'd read in Psalms, God had literally given him an "escape from death."

When the truck pulled back into Arenal late Saturday night, the news spread like wildfire. "The preacher is alive! He's walking! He's healed!"

The next day, the church was packed for the Sunday morning service. Scores more peered through the doors and windows, wanting to see this walking miracle. Marcelino read the verse God had given him from Psalm 68:20, then testified, "By God's saving power, I have escaped from death and stand before you alive."

Many accepted Jesus as Lord and Savior that day. In a town considered hard and unchangeable, God used Marcelino's accident as a visible witness to the reality of Jesus. After that Sunday morning, the church saw steady growth, and God opened many doors for ongoing witness in that town.

Chapter Twenty-Eight
Ouch, My Band-Aid

It wasn't the cut on Luis's thumb that caused the problem. It was the band-aid. Luis's wife Eliet, one of my close friends in Costa Rica, shared this story with our home church congregation. Her husband Luis had been repairing a staircase in their little house when he accidentally hit his thumb with the hammer instead of the steel nail. His thumb bled and turned black, so he wrapped it with a band-aid.

Luis was employed by Costa Rica's largest milk processing plant, where he worked a night shift in the powdered milk department. That night while he was processing a tank of powdered milk, his bloodied band-aid fell off his thumb into the tank. The huge container of white powder was far too deep to begin looking for the band-aid. It was gone!

This was a catastrophe for Luis's family. A thousand thoughts rushed through his mind. If the band-aid was discovered in someone's powdered milk and reported, the reputation of this high-quality product would be in serious jeopardy. Luis had been working alone that night, so an inspection would show that the band-aid had to come from him. If he confessed, the batch could be pulled from circulation, but it would waste thousands of gallons of milk and he'd be dismissed from his job, leaving his family without an income. That meant no rice and beans to feed his wife and five children, no uniforms for the children's schooling, no rent money for their house.

The next morning when his shift had ended, Luis returned home with a heavy heart. His facial expression immediately told Eliet something was wrong. He related what had happened at work.

"Honey, there's no human way out of this," she responded. "So let's pray."

The couple knelt together and cried out to God, "You have never failed us since we put our trust in You. Now we're in trouble. We don't have the answer. God, please help us. We are committing this band-aid to You, trusting You will solve this problem."

Days passed by, then weeks. Always a faithful, hardworking employee, Luis continued working to the best of his ability. The company processed thousands of cans and plastic bags of powdered milk daily, supplying the national demand as well as exports to other countries, but nothing was said or noticed about a bloodied band-aid turning up in the product.

As a bonus to the monthly paycheck, the milk processing company gave each of its hundreds of employees a can of powdered milk to take home for their families. One month later, Eliet opened the latest free can to prepare breakfast for her children. On top of the snow-white powder, she spotted something dark and wadded-up that most certainly didn't belong

Chapter Twenty-Eight: Ouch, My Band-Aid

there. Was it a cockroach? No, it couldn't be! Yes, it was indeed Luis's ugly bloodied band-aid!

Eliet cried and thanked God at the same time. As she showed Luis what she'd found and the couple explained this incredible miracle to their children, their humble home became a chapel of praise. God had supernaturally delivered the very powdered milk containing that ugly band-aid to their home. Together, the family praised God for His mercy and wonderful care. Luis continued on at the milk processing plant, maintaining a great work record.

The stories of God's divine working during our time in Costa Rica are endless. Another involved Vietnam war veteran Dave Roever. My husband had invited him to Costa Rica to share his unique testimony. His disfiguration made him easy to identify as he exited from the San Jose airport immigration check.

Dave had been serving in Vietnam with the U.S. Navy special warfare division when a bullet striking his hand caused a white phosphorus grenade to explode just as he was about to throw it. He was burned beyond recognition and pronounced dead several times, but God miraculously saved him. He received numerous military awards including the prestigious Purple Heart. His gift of communication, faith in Christ, and amazing recovery later served as a platform to share his testimony with U.S. troops around the world, youth conferences, and national TV talk shows. Dave and his wife also founded Eagles Summit Ranch in Colorado, where they helped American troops and others recover from traumatic injuries.

We enjoyed the week Dave spent with our family in Costa Rica. He showed us before and after photos reflecting his painful journey. Though he only had five remaining fingers, he played the piano beautifully "by ear," a joke he liked to make as he took off an artificial ear to play. Each night, we took David to a different AG church plant where Bill translated his incredible testimony. Very quickly seeing past his visible injuries to the love and compassion Dave displayed for them, the Costa Ricans gave him the name "Brother Love."

In another town called Escazu, Bill and I knew our planned evangelistic conference would involve a spiritual battle. Escazu was known in Costa Rica for its occult activity. Newspapers advertised fetishes for sale to protect houses from earthquakes. The rented meeting place was a movie theater, and the owner wouldn't allow us to take down obscene ads on the walls. But we had faith that God would reveal Himself in this dark, wicked town.

Shortly before the first service, we were praying together when a girl entered the movie theater and began ripping up seats screwed to the floor, throwing them around the salon with superhuman strength. Before we could reach her, police officers rushed in and arrested her. We learned that she was a drug dealer and involved in the occult like many local people trapped in Satan's deceitful snares.

We started the conference with little response. An evil shield seemed to keep us from reaching people's hearts. But during the final service on Pentecost Sunday, we witnessed a major spiritual breakthrough. At least two hundred people attended the meeting. Many accepted Christ, and twenty-two received God's gift of the

Chapter Twenty-Eight: Ouch, My Band-Aid

Holy Spirit. These new believers formed the core of a Spirit-filled church plant in Escazu.

Several months later we received a letter postmarked Bangor, Maine, that read:

Dear Brother Bradney, I am a church deacon. I recently started interceding in prayer. A few months ago, I had an unusual experience. I'm writing to find out if it came from God. One night I was awakened and saw your face. You were standing with an outstretched Bible encircled by demonic powers. They resisted your efforts to preach. I knew I needed to pray, though it was difficult to get out of my warm bed. I prayed until I saw that ring of demonic power broken. Tell me, was this experience of God?

When Bill checked the date of this experience, he discovered that this deacon had been roused from bed to pray the night before Pentecost Sunday when God had poured out His Spirit. With great joy and thankfulness, we wrote back to the deacon, "Brother, you were right on! If the Lord again challenges you to pray, please obey."

Today Escazu has many growing Spirit-filled churches. A deacon's prayer in Maine changed a demonic, occultic stronghold thousands of miles away in Costa Rica.

Chapter Twenty-Nine

Five Dollars and a Heavenly Father

In 1980, we once again returned to the United States for furlough, staying in a guest apartment at the Overseas Ministries Study Center in Ventnor, New Jersey. While sharing our ministry with churches and reconnecting with family and friends, we received a surprise letter from Bangalore, India, informing us that my dad would arrive in New York City in just three days.

Though delighted to see him after so many years, we didn't know how we'd meet him at Kennedy International Airport, since Bill was on a speaking trip with our only vehicle. Checking his schedule, Bill discovered that his speaking engagement the night before Dad's arrival was just a couple of miles from Kennedy International Airport. He had the following two days free, so he could meet Dad and drive him to our furlough home. Only God could have coordinated my husband's and father's schedules so perfectly.

After years since his last trip from India, Dad's clothing was all very threadbare, and we discovered he'd arrived with only five dollars in his wallet. We offered to buy him a new suit and shoes to wear when speaking at American churches, but he emphatically refused to let us spend our funds on him. So we suggested a visit

Chapter Twenty-Nine: Five Dollars and a Heavenly Father

to a nearby church second-hand clothing boutique where we and other furloughing missionaries from tropical countries routinely found winter clothing to get us through the American winters.

Dad agreed. In God's gracious provision, we found two brand-new men's suits at the boutique with price tags still attached that were exactly Dad's size and even his favorite colors. We also found good-quality shoes and shirts with matching ties. Such finds among the used clothes typically donated to the boutique was most unusual.

As Dad ministered at a local AG church that Sunday, the congregation was greatly impacted by God's anointed Word. He also looked great. Consistent with Dad's life of ministry in India and around the world, we'd witnessed once again that God isn't limited to five dollars in our pocket. He divinely plans and provides as we obey Him. Dad was eventually buried in one of those suits, by then well-worn.

As mentioned, our furlough housing was just two blocks from the Atlantic Ocean. Bill was on the road speaking when we received weather warnings of an approaching hurricane. I wanted the children to experience God's power and majesty, so we ventured outside, holding tightly to each other in the strong winds. Massive waves roared and crashed against the nearby retaining wall, and the wind grew so powerful that we were walking almost horizontally. We finally had to grip the boardwalk fence to pull ourselves home, by then totally drenched.

Reflecting later on this adventure, two of our children described it as "awesome." The other pointed out quite accurately, "Mom, that was so dangerous!"

Our year of furlough came to an end. We faced some painful farewells as for the first time we'd be returning to Costa Rica without all three of our children. Now nineteen, Ruth had finished her first year of college at Southeastern College, later renamed Southeastern University, in Lakeland, FL, where she would be returning in the fall. A much more difficult parting was with our seventeen-year-old son Phil, who was not walking with the Lord. During his last two years in Costa Rica, his popularity in his international school had led him to choose inappropriate friends.

Another negative factor was our attitude toward his love for soccer, which we came to regret. Since sports was not in my own background, I didn't understand that Phil needed our support of his athletic involvement. Bill was so busy ministering that soccer wasn't on his priority list either. Concerned about our family's future, Bill called a family conference. We expressed that we'd willing to stay in the United States if this would help our children.

But our children all agreed that Bill and I should return to Costa Rica with Cheryl. Ruth was settled for the near future at Southeastern College. Meanwhile, an opportunity had opened for Phil attend Ben Lippen High School, a Christian boarding school for missionary kids in Asheville, North Carolina. Phil was excited at the prospect while Bill and I felt that a structured Christian atmosphere, high academic standard, and lots of fun with other Christian young people would benefit our son in this critical time of his life.

Chapter Twenty-Nine: Five Dollars and a Heavenly Father

Phil along with Bill's parents, sister, and brother-in-law joined us at the airport to see us off on our flight back to Costa Rica. Before we boarded, Bill prayed earnestly for Phil, speaking over him the command of Jesus in Matthew 6:33: "Seek first the Kingdom of God . . . and all these things shall be added." (NKJV)

We hugged goodbye, then headed down the long corridor to our gate. As we obeyed God's call back to Costa Rica, we were trusting Him to care for Phil's spiritual wellbeing. But that didn't erase the pain we felt as we walked away from our precious son.

"Don't worry about me!" Phil called after us. "I can take care of myself!"

That was precisely the challenge. He didn't want to submit to Christ's lordship.

Back in Costa Rica, our lives quickly filled up again with ministry. As the year came to a close, the pastor of our home church in San Jose asked Bill to speak at the New Year's Eve service. Every pew was filled and young people sat on the platform and altar steps as Bill challenged us all to faithfully love and serve our Lord during the coming year.

But as young people responded to Bill's challenge, his heart cried out: *God, thank you for these precious Costa Ricans sincerely offering their hearts and talents to you. But where is my son? In some wild party? This is New Year's Eve! Please speak to Phil's heart!*

It was well after midnight before we were back home. At 3 a.m., Bill and I were just falling asleep when the ring of the telephone startled us. When Bill answered it, an operator stated, "This is a collect call from Philip Bradney. Will you accept charges?"

Our first thought was that Phil was in some kind of trouble. Urgently, Bill asked, "What's wrong, Phil?"

"Nothing, Dad!" Phil responded with evident emotion. "For the first time, everything is right!"

Phil went on to share that a Ben Lippen classmate he'd begun dating named Karen had invited him to hear missionary author Elizabeth Elliot at her home church. During the service, God had spoken strongly to Phil, and he'd surrendered his life to God. Karen eventually became our wonderful, loving daughter-in-law, and Phil's life-changing commitment to Christ continues today.

It was the best New Year's Day celebration we could ever have. God faithfully fulfills His promise when we seek first His Kingdom.

Chapter Thirty

More Student God-Encounters

We continued to be encouraged by the life stories and God-encounters of our students. As Bill and I taught at the AG Bible Institute in San Jose during the early 1980s, we witnessed a student named Sandra study diligently and grow spiritually. When classes weren't in session, she taught, evangelized, encouraged, and prayed in nearly every section of Costa Rica. She shared with me her following life story.

On New Year's Eve, nineteen-year-old Sandra and her friends danced wildly to the high-pitched beat of rock music and celebrated the new year with drugs, alcohol, and cigarettes. But Sandra felt completely alone. Her boyfriend was furious because she wouldn't fulfill his desire for physical intimacy. With bleary eyes, she looked out over the majestic Caribbean coastline of her seaside hometown. The moon shone on the white crests of ocean waves, and stars sparkled like diamonds on the black velvet backdrop of the night sky. Palms swayed gracefully in the gentle tropical breeze.

If God made this world so beautiful, Sandra mused, *why am I so ugly?*

Do Angels Wear Overalls?

She reflected on her past. Her parents had abandoned her when she was eighteen months old. She'd lived with a series of relatives, never knowing if anyone really loved her. She always felt like an intruder, so at the age of twelve she'd finally given up and started taking drugs, seeking some fulfilment. The drugs soon dominated her, and she began stealing to support her habit. Her sloppy, faded blue jeans and straggly hair reflected her inner confusion and hopelessness.

Then came that New Year's night when she found herself high on drugs and alone with God's beautiful Caribbean creation. She began mulling over Christian programs she'd heard on Trans World Radio as a little girl that spoke of a God of love. How could God love her when He'd let her grow up with so much hate and sin?

Acutely aware of her sinfulness, Sandra cried out desperately, "God, if You really exist and if You love me, please take away my hate and emptiness. Please forgive me and make me beautiful!"

At that moment, a miracle took place. Generally, Sandra remained high for several hours after taking drugs, but within a few minutes her mind was completely clear. As she cried before the Lord, He cleansed her sin and hatred, replacing it with His love. Her world looked completely different. When she awoke the next morning, she was still filled with a joy she wanted to share with everyone.

That Sunday morning, Sandra was on a stroll enjoying her transformed world when she heard lively music. It was coming from an Assemblies of God church, and the song lyrics spoke of how faith in Jesus can save a sinner. Entering, she listened to the music and pastor preaching. Everything seemed so strange yet beautiful. At the altar call, she publicly accepted Christ as her Savior. She returned that night for the evening service.

During the next week, cigarette smoke nauseated her. She threw her cigarettes away. She realized she didn't need them or drugs. Two weeks later in her bedroom as she praised the Lord, she suddenly began speaking a language she'd never learned. That evening before the church service, she asked her pastor what had happened.

"Jesus filled you with His Holy Spirit to make you an effective witness for Him," he explained.

Thrilled, Sandra volunteered to clean church floors and bathrooms. Later she told the pastor, "I want to do more!"

He suggested she share her story in her neighborhood. From house to house and in the streets, she began sharing the good news that Jesus could change others as He had changed her. As she continued to grow spiritually, her pastor advised her to consider attending the Bible Institute, which she did.

One day while studying at the Bible Institute, Sandra shared with me her desire to teach God's Word in a needy country. Together we prayed for God's leading. After her graduation, the Costa Rica AG general superintendent invited her to teach in a Spanish Bible Institute in Orange Walk, Belize, where a Costa Rican couple served as the first appointed and supported missionaries from the Costa Rican AG churches.

Sandra was delighted. She expressed to me, "I feel I'm in harmony with God and His people. At last I feel beautiful. He made me beautiful to bring Him glory."

Eighteen-year-old Eduardo from Nicaragua also shared his story with me. His sister and brother-in-law were both Bible Institute students. As an adolescent in Nicaragua, he was extremely violent, sometimes foaming from his mouth and controlled by a destructive demonic force. His family was afraid of him.

His grandmother lived next door. She loved Jesus. She prayed with and for Eduardo, took him to church, and read the Bible to him. Although he was rebellious, Eduardo loved his grandmother and knew that she loved him dearly. When he was sixteen, his grandmother died. This caused Eduardo to begin thinking about life after death. He knew his grandmother was with Jesus whom she had so faithfully served.

Eduardo graduated from high school and studied at night to be an accountant while working during the day for a government agency. When a socialist party took control of Nicaragua, Eduardo was excited by the revolutionary government's promises of peace, prosperity, and a better life for poor people. But the government soon began instituting communistic policies that resulted in hunger, poverty, fear, and bondage for the Nicaraguan people.

One Friday morning, Eduardo's father told him, "Son, I feel you shouldn't go to work today."

Eduardo stayed home. He later discovered that government authorities had come to his work complex to forcibly take him and other young men into military service. He didn't want to fight for this communist regime, but he didn't know how to avoid it. Some of his friends had shot themselves in the arm or leg to make themselves unfit for military service. But Eduardo didn't want to risk that.

He hid for twenty-two days at a friend's house. Meanwhile, his sister at the Bible Institute in San Jose along with other Christian family members prayed that he could escape. Through many miracles, he managed to purchase an airline ticket to San Jose. Passing through airport immigration, he prayed silently that God would keep the guards from stopping him and turning him in to the military authorities.

The guard looked through his legal documents and ticket, then brusquely ordered, "Go ahead."

Eduardo let out a sigh of relief. God had answered his prayer, and he was finally safe. When the plane landed, Eduardo's sister and her husband were there to welcome him. As they took him to the Assemblies of God Bible Institute, he watched with wonder the young men playing soccer in the streets without fear of being grabbed by the military. He no longer had to hide or worry about who might following him. He was free.

At the Bible Institute, Eduardo witnessed other young people his age worshipping and studying God's Word. Trying to process all he observed, he concluded: *God has blessed me with freedom. I am indebted to Him. I must give Him my life.*

Kneeling beside his sister in the chapel, Eduardo accepted Jesus as his Savior and Lord. He was so happy to be absolutely free spiritually as well as politically. From that day on, he dedicated his energy, hours, and talents to share God's goodness with others.

Chapter Thirty-One

God's Divine Timing

The international president of Women's Aglow Fellowship (now Aglow International) attended a Central American Women's Aglow convention in Costa Rica when I shared the Word. We became acquainted through this event, and she invited me to speak at the 1984 Aglow national conventions in Denver, Colorado, and Knoxville, Tennessee.

I felt this was God-programmed, so I talked to Bill, who volunteered to cover my teaching responsibilities if I received permission from our mission agency. Our director gave me the green light, and I confirmed my participation. I also wanted to visit our three children, all of whom were now in the United States. Our oldest daughter Ruth was now married and living with her husband in Lakeland, Florida. Our son Phil was at King's College, a Christian liberal arts college in New York City. Our youngest, Cheryl, was attending Ben Lippen High School in Asheville, North Carolina.

I was planning for this trip when Bill and I received the exciting news that Ruth and her husband were expecting their first child. Looking over my calendar, I realized that my lay-over in Florida could possibly coincide with our first grandson's birth.

In God's perfect timing, I arrived in Florida the very night Ruth went into labor. The next day darling Bobby was born. I was able to cradle God's precious gift to our family and help Ruth during her first mother days. I left for the Aglow convention in Denver, Colorado, praising God for arranging the timing of my visit with my first grandchild's birth.

Since the Denver hotel room I'd been assigned was double-occupancy, I invited my sister Pauline to join me. She travelled from Big Fork, Montana, where she and her husband pastored a church. In between dynamic services, we enjoyed wonderful sister time together.

The views from the huge glass windows of the Denver convention center where the Aglow conference was being hosted gave breathtaking testimony to God's glory. As I sat on the platform waiting to speak, I could see the sun shimmering on majestic snow-capped Rocky Mountain peaks. Their beauty affirmed the song from the Psalms that the women were singing about the earth being full of God's glory (Psalm 72:19).

But despite the beauty and worshipful music, I was worried and tense. Silently, I conversed with God. *Yes, God, I see the earth full of Your glory. But here is a little piece of earth desperately needing Your glory. Remember, Lord, that I'm the giggler! In Latin America, I feel at home speaking because they know I love them and I know they'll excuse my mistakes. But here are hundreds of women I've never seen before coming from all over the United States. They've paid a high price to be here in this luxurious hotel. Lord, if You don't fill me with Your glory, I don't know if I can get to my feet to speak!*

At that moment, a young violinist quietly left the orchestra. Walking over to me, she bent down and whispered, "I just want you to know you are a chosen earthen vessel God is filling with His glory to proclaim His Word."

Wow, what an immediate answer from God! Tears of gratefulness washed away my doubts as I confidently stood to share what God had given me for these dear women. Later when I was in the elevator heading up to my hotel room, another woman in the elevator asked, "Aren't you the person who spoke this evening at the Aglow convention?"

"Yes, I am," I responded.

Giving me a tight hug, she said, "I loved what you shared, and I saw God's glory all over you!"

I was humbled to think that God would fill a defective, weak clay pot like me to bring Him glory and make evident that the all-surpassing power of God's message is from God and not God's servants (2 Corinthians 4:7).

Philip's girlfriend Karen was also attending King's College. The two of them picked me up at the airport and drove me to the college. Karen graciously gave up her bed for me while she slept on the floor. It was a special joy to get to know Karen as well as her parents. She later became our fun-loving, God-serving daughter-in-love.

"Where is your next convention?" Phil asked me.

"Knoxville, Tennessee," I answered.

Chapter Thirty-One: God's Divine Timing

"That's only a couple hours' drive from Ben Lippen," Phil pointed out.

We checked the map. Then I called Cheryl and asked, "Would you join me in a double-occupancy hotel room in Knoxville, Tennessee, where I'm speaking at an Aglow convention?"

Cheryl was ecstatic to join me in Knoxville. Her bubbly personality blessed everyone she met, and we enjoyed special mother-daughter moments together laughing, sharing, and shopping in between services. When I finally returned to Costa Rica, my heart was overflowing with gratitude to my heavenly Father. Only God could have planned a fulfilling ministry trip that included free-of-charge visits with each of our three dear children, our first grandchild, my sister, and even our future daughter-in-law. From beginning to end, it was truly a loving and gracious demonstration of God's perfect divine timing!

Chapter Thirty-Two

Beauty from Ugliness

Our Bible Institute cook and dear friend Vera was faithfully and lovingly married for many years to the Bible Institute caretaker Gerardo. God blessed them with two healthy children before he passed away in 1980 at the young age of thirty-five.

Though Gerardo's wife was a devout follower of Jesus and Gerardo was well acquainted with the gospel, he'd been unwilling to commit his life to Christ's lordship. God spoke to him through a vision, but its impact lasted only a few days. Testimonies of Bible Institute faculty and students constantly reminded him of Jesus's transforming power, but Gerardo continued to reject that transforming power for his own life.

When Gerardo fell ill, doctors first diagnosed his pain as a severe nervous condition. Later they discovered advanced aggressive cancer in his liver. Gerardo responded to medical treatment. While in the hospital, he also reflected on his wasted life. Finally, he asked God to forgive him and became His child. When he returned home, both family and friends immediately noted his changed attitude and habits.

Chapter Thirty-Two: Beauty from Ugliness

In time, Gerardo became ill again. It was confirmed that his cancer had returned, and the specialist advised him that he had no more than a month to live. He spent that time with family and friends, reading the Bible, praying, as well as enjoying and praising God. When Bill and I visited Gerardo in his bedroom, we sensed God's presence and could see God's glory reflected in his face. Although his body was deteriorating, his spirit seemed close to Jesus, and being with him felt like a taste of heaven.

Angels escorted Gerardo home to heaven. At his funeral, scores of non-believers heard how Gerardo had experienced God's gracious forgiveness. Five years later, I accompanied his wife Vera to witness the exhumation of Gerardo's remains. This was not uncommon in Costa Rica where cemetery plots were typically rented rather than purchased permanently. Due to the high rental cost, caskets were exhumed after five years and the remains transferred to a two-foot long box that would be reburied in a much smaller plot.

Vera and I both dreaded what awaited us, so we tried to focus on God's goodness as we drove. We reminded each other that God's master plan is always for His glory and our well-being, even with a life cut so short as Gerardo's. We stopped to buy potted yellow mums from a roadside flower stand.

When we arrived at the cemetery, a workman with pick and shovel unearthed the casket. The wood was in good condition, but the metal hinges and handles were rusted. As the workman pried open the lid, I embraced Vera tightly. Our eyes filled with tears and pain at what we saw. Gerardo's wine-colored corduroy trousers, gray floral shirt, and beige socks were still intact, but the flesh was gone from the bones. The skull lay there, the jaw dislocated. Long hair had fallen on the pillow, and loose teeth with some gold fillings lay on the shirt. Long fingernails hung loosely from finger bones, and a horrid smell penetrated the air.

Joining us, the cemetery manager commented, "I wish every proud, rich person could observe what we see. From the moment of death, money, houses, prestige, clothes, and education have little importance. Bodies of the famous and homeless face the same destiny. They all return to dust."

"That is true," I agreed. "But for those who love Jesus, God gives the real person an abundant entrance into His divine presence. That isn't the real Gerardo, just the remains of his earthly house. Because he accepted Jesus as his Savior, God welcomed him to his eternal home five years ago where he is enjoying the beauty of Jesus's presence."

I could see this perspective was a comfort to Vera. The cemetery worker slowly and carefully placed each of Gerardo's bones into the new smaller wooden box and nailed it securely. We followed as he buried it again in another section of the cemetery. Vera placed the potted yellow mums on top of the freshly turned earth of the new burial site.

As we returned home, Vera and I spoke of heaven, loved ones who have gone before us, and most of all our Lord and Savior. Together we prayed that we would not be so occupied with our earthly house that we failed to live each day with an eternal perspective. We wanted to hear Jesus welcome us home as promised in Scripture: "Well done, good and faithful servant . . . Enter into the joy of your Lord" (Matthew 25:21 NKJV).

Chapter Thirty-Two: Beauty from Ugliness

Five years after Gerardo's death, his body was reduced to dust and bones. But the real Gerardo was enjoying abundant, eternal life with Jesus.

Another story that happened around this time made me very angry and outraged—at least at the time. One day very early in the morning, I drove to the bottom of a big hill on the outskirts of San Jose along with Sylvia, the teenaged daughter of missionary colleagues. From there we climbed a muddy hillside.

The reason for our visit was to find how many children lived up on this hillside who might be potential students for a new Christian school being built nearby thanks to the generosity of American believers. The school would provide a biblically-based education, uniforms, medical attention, and a nutritious noon meal.

When we reached the top of the hill, Sylvia and I were stunned to see the poverty and terrible living conditions. Shacks cobbled together with whatever was available housed mostly mothers with young children. There were no roads, running water, or electricity. To get to the closest school on another hill, children had to slide down the steep hill, then ford a dangerously fast-flowing stream. One child had already drowned while trying to wade across the strong current.

As we noted children's names and ages, the mothers were grateful and excited to hear about the possibility of a Christian school. One mother told her daughter to show us the doll God had given her in answer to her prayers. She explained that Maria had been praying faithfully for a doll, but her job as a maid barely provided one meal a day for her three children. Though her mother dearly wished she could grant her daughter's wish, there was no money for toys.

Then one afternoon while hauling water from the river, Maria saw something strange poking up out of the community trash pile. It looked like an arm. Digging around, she quickly unearthed a battered doll. Its face was disfigured, and it had only one arm and part of a leg. But Maria carefully shook off the dirt and cradled the doll in her arms, thanking God that He'd heard her prayer.

Hurrying home with her treasure, Maria imagined this much-injured doll's story. *You disobeyed your mother and crossed a city street without looking both ways. A car hit you. With no one to help, you were left disabled. But now I will take care of you.*

Maria proudly showed Sylvia and me her doll wrapped in a rag blanket. I did my best to admire it, though it was the ugliest doll I'd ever seen. But as Sylvia and I trudged back down the hill and drove home, I was angry and heartbroken to have witnessed the tragedy of so many mothers trying to defend and care for their children with so little.

As I changed out of my muddy clothes, I cried out to God. *It's not fair, God. Maria prayed for a doll. If I had been You, I would have given her a pretty one with hair to braid and a frilly dress. Just look at the doll You gave her!*

Then I felt God respond to my critical outburst. *Maria asked me for a doll. I gave her a doll. She is caring for her doll. I love Maria. I'm preparing her not to care for dolls but for real people with deep hurts and needs.*

Chapter Thirty-Two: Beauty from Ugliness

Broken, I asked God's forgiveness for misjudging Him and His good gifts and accepted with humility the life lesson He'd just taught me. The next year on furlough in the United States, I told the doll story to a children's Sunday school class. Deeply touched, a little girl who lived next to the church ran home and returned with a beautiful doll.

"I want Maria to have my favorite doll," she told me excitedly. "Will you take it to her?"

I was delighted to do so. Many years later in 2005 when I was a professor at Valley Forge Christian College, I again shared my ugly doll story to freshmen enjoying dessert in our home on their first day of classes. A girl spoke up. "Sister Hilda, I know the girl who gave you that doll to take back for Maria. She is a close friend of mine and told me that story. She is now a student right here at VFCC preparing for Christian service."

Chapter Thirty-Three

Adios, Costa Rica

Bill and I both loved the Costa Rican people and felt loved. We'd seen an explosion of God's good news in both the capital and in rural communities. But our dear colleagues and field leaders Bill and Hope Brooke, now speaking and teaching in many Latin American countries, often shared their burden when they returned to Costa Rica. "God is working in such a marked way in Costa Rica. There are other countries with desperate needs."

As Bill and I listened to them, we began conversing seriously together. "The work here has capable leadership of both nationals and missionaries. Our children are grown and in the United States. We are both healthy. Let's consider investing our remaining years of ministry in a more needy country."

We wrote our area director. He referred us to our missions director, who was elated at the possibility of our moving to a new country. Bill and I began learning the history of injustice, war, poverty, and resistance to the gospel in land-locked Paraguay, South America. As throughout Latin America, God was changing the evangelical landscape of that country. Just in the last four years from 1984-1987, the Assemblies of God church family there had

Chapter Thirty-Three: Adios, Costa Rica

grown over a thousand percent. Hundreds were finding God's purpose for living and being healed.

As a consequence, the need for trained Bible teachers and ministry leaders was great. A new red-brick AG Theological Institute had been constructed in the capital city of Asuncion and needed a director. We soon received an invitation from the Paraguayan national church for Bill to direct the school. They also asked if I would direct Paraguay's AG Impact office, which was the hub for scores of short-term teachers, volunteers, construction teams, etc.

Although it was painful to say good-bye to the Costa Ricans and missionary colleagues we'd grown to love and appreciate, we felt that God leading us in this new adventure to Paraguay.

That furlough in 1986, Bill was invited to serve as missionary-in-residence at Central Bible College in Springfield, Missouri, teaching missions courses to hundreds of young people eagerly seeking God's will for their lives. Our daughter Ruth and her family had moved from Lakeland, FL, to Springfield, so we enjoyed getting to know our first grandson Bobby, a toddler at the time. Simultaneously, Bill and I dedicated a semester for advanced study at the Assemblies of God Theological Seminary. In 1987, I graduated with honors in a Master of Arts degree.

One of Bill's students at CBC, Terry had found herself questioning God's love. She'd married a young man named Norbert, who was the music and worship director of a Wisconsin church. The two enjoyed a warm marriage relationship nurtured by their mutual love for God and each other, but they felt one thing lacking. Terry and Norbert wanted children, but after three years of infertility, tests showed one chance in a thousand of conceiving.

A prayer warrior in their church received a word from God that Terry would conceive in May 1985. That is exactly what happened, but just four months into the pregnancy, she suffered a miscarriage and lost the baby. Confused and heartbroken, she cried out to God, *Why would you miraculously allow me to conceive only to take our baby?*

Though they didn't understand, Terry and her husband chose to trust God's plan for their lives. They celebrated a second honeymoon in the beautiful Rocky Mountains of Canada's Banff National Park, clinging to each other and to God. Returning home, they put away all baby clothes and dreams of a child.

That following December, Terry received a phone call mid-morning asking why her husband Norbert hadn't arrived at work. When she couldn't track him down, Terry called the police to begin a missing persons search. It was only a few hours later that she was informed her husband's car had been found with her husband deceased behind the wheel. To lose a young husband so soon after her baby was a great shock. Terry felt as though she'd undergone major surgery and part of her was now missing.

Lord, do you really love me? she cried out to God. *First my baby and now my dear husband!*

For the next year, Terry grieved intensely. She wished she could die and join her husband and daughter in heaven. But as she cried out to God, He comforted her. She dug deeply into her Bible, and God's Word sustained her. She gradually learned to say *I* again

Chapter Thirty-Three: Adios, Costa Rica

instead of *we*. In lonely night hours, she learned to recognize her Savior's gentle voice, and He became a heavenly husband to the grieving widow. As she submitted every decision to His guidance, Jesus daily gave her life and love.

The following year after losing husband and baby, Terry enrolled in Central Bible College. She'd thought she was strong enough to handle being so far away from family and friends. But the loneliness roused her deep grief, and she once again found herself crying uncontrollably.

Then a college friend invited Terry to a student fellowship at our furlough home. After a meal of delicious Mexican food, we all came together for worship. A visiting professor who had never met Terry shared a word from the Holy Spirit that someone in the room was suffering from a broken heart. He went on, "Jesus invites you to give Him each broken piece, and He will make your heart whole."

Terry knew God was speaking directly to her. She burst out crying as she gave Him her shattered heart. God started healing her emotionally as she sat in His divine presence. The next morning, she took her place singing in choir with a new song welling up from a healed heart. Afterwards, classmates asked her, "Terry, what happened? Your face was glowing today!"

Later that semester, Terry heard about a ministry trip to Mexico City that Bill and I were co-leading with another faculty member during spring break. She wanted to go, but reservations had long been filled. Then Bill had to cancel his participation because his dad had fallen ill. This made a vacancy for Terry.

In route to the airport, Terry and I discussed with two young men on the Mexico City team the joy of marrying in God's will. Over the course of the ministry trip, Terry developed a friendship with one of those young men, Don Bader. That summer, they both served together in short-term missions in Nairobi, Africa. In August they were married.

Terry's life hadn't worked out as she'd originally planned. But when those she so deeply loved were stripped from her, Jesus remained steadfast. He became more precious with each passing day, giving her more than she could have dreamed or planned. She could confidently say, "Yes, Jesus loves me!"

Dr. Don and Terry Bader went on enjoy a great marriage, and God gave them two wonderful daughters. They have served as home missionaries to Asian university students and professors in Wisconsin. Dr. Don also teaches yearly intense short-term leadership courses in other Asian countries.

Chapter Thirty-Four

Starting Again

In January 1988, Bill and I arrived in Paraguay, a small landlocked country well below the equator in southern South America. It seemed as if we were on another planet from Costa Rica. While the official language was still Spanish, just about everything else was different—their accent, sayings, government, world view, diet, climate, terrain, architecture, dress codes, racial background, and history. Instead of a peaceful democracy, Paraguay had been governed for over three decades by an authoritarian dictator, Alfredo Stroessner. The majority of the population were Guarani, a major lowland Indian tribe greatly discriminated against by the ruling Spanish aristocracy.

Though we'd never visited the country and didn't know a soul there, we soon developed close relationships and effective ministry. We learned new places, customs, sayings, and driving through busy intersections without stop signs or traffic signals. We also learned new foods and drinks like freshly baked *chipa*, a delicious corn bread sold by street vendors, and *mate*, a highly caffeinated tea drunk instead of coffee out of silver straws from hollowed-out gourds.

Over the six years before our arrival, forty Assemblies of God tent campaigns had resulted in numerous church plants, three new Christian elementary schools, and the new Theological Institute in the capital city of Asuncion. But many Paraguayan towns and villages still remained without an evangelical witness. Bill took over the directorship of the Theological Institute while I coordinated short-term missions, evangelizing, long-distance teaching, and construction teams. Bill and I both taught classes as well in the Theological Institute.

Edith was one of my students during our first year in Asuncion. Hate and bitterness had poisoned this timid young woman like a suffocating, growing tumor. She hadn't seen or heard from her mother in four years. But during the Christmas holidays in 1988, everything changed.

By age three, Edith was caring for her one-year-old brother while her mother and nine-year-old sister Felicia worked. Another sister somewhat older than Edith named Isabel lived with a relative. One day her baby brother, already sick with diarrhea, began vomiting. With no doctor or other help at hand, the child died, leaving Edith feeling guilty about his death. Her mother soon had another baby boy, Celso, with her latest boyfriend, whom Edith and her sister were required to call Papá (Dad).

As a teen, Edith's mother had practiced witchcraft and tried to drown her sinful life by drinking. Edith was petrified when dishes danced in their house due to demonic activity. Her mother would scream, claiming she was seeing ghosts in the patio. She finally left her boyfriend when he tried to rape Edith's sister Felicia.

Chapter Thirty-Four: Starting Again

They later lived in Port Pinasco, a busy port town on the Paraguay River. When a boat captain named Porfirio asked Edith's mom to be his mistress, she abandoned the children and moved onto his boat. The siblings were left to fend for themselves and suffered miserably for lack of food.

A year later, Edith's mother suddenly returned to take fourteen-year-old Felicia and baby Celso with her. She forced Felicia to become an older man's mistress in exchange for money and clothes. Edith was sent to join her older sister Isabel living with a cruel woman who beat them and fed them on dog scraps. Edith felt lonely and unloved, often crying herself to sleep. During the day, she tried to forget her ugly life by living in a fantasy world.

Eventually, the sisters moved back in with their mother and her boyfriend Porfirio. When Porfirio was drunk, he beat the children and threatened Edith's mom. He carried a gun and knife. Finally after a big argument, Edith's mother left him. Edith was relieved, but her mother soon found another male friend.

By the time she was nine years old, Edith had come to the realization that her mother was simply a bad person. This made her increasingly angry, especially when her mother again abandoned Isabel, Celso, and Edith, leaving them to walk the streets looking for something to eat and to sleep out in the open, huddled together in fear.

They eventually found their mother with another man named Alonso. At first, he seemed kind and fed the children, but soon there were fights and jealousy. Edith's mother left Alonso to live with another man who didn't work. Edith and her sister Isabel had to peddle fruit on the streets to support their family.

Edith had come to hate her mother. All the bad experiences with her mother's boyfriends also left her hating men in general. Her sister Isabel became her only friend and security. At twelve, Edith began attempting suicide, taking poison, and cutting herself. She received many sexual propositions from men, but she refused them, determined not to follow her mother's example.

When Edith was fourteen, the family moved to Paraguay's capital, Asuncion. Their neighbor, a Christian, told Edith that God loved her. She'd never heard those words before. Alone at night, she thought about God. For the first time, she felt God's love expressed through this neighbor's kindness, including inviting the hungry young teen over for meals. Edith longed to stay in this kind woman's peaceful house instead of her own.

One day Edith asked her neighbor if she could go with her to church. That Sunday as Edith entered the little church building with her neighbor, she felt as though she'd entered heaven. There was beautiful, joyous singing. When the worship leader asked visitors to stand, she timidly forced herself up. Many people hugged her. She felt loved. At the altar call, she repeated the sinner's prayer with the pastor. She felt different inside and had a smile on her face as they walked home.

By this point, Isabel had moved to another city, and their oldest sister Felicia was long gone. Edith was working as a maid during the day and going to school at night. One day when she returned home from work, her mother hurried out of the house

Chapter Thirty-Four: Starting Again

without greeting Edith. When Edith went inside, she found a strange man sitting on her bed. He tried to rape her, but she fought back with all her strength and managed to escape. Screaming, she ran down the street until she spotted her mother.

"Why did you leave me alone with that man?" she demanded.

"Because I wanted to," her mother replied curtly. Edith realized her mother was trying to do to her what she'd done with her older sister Felicia, trading her daughter's virtue for financial gain. This made her hate her mother even more.

Edith was so happy when her Christian neighbor asked her to work in her home. The kindly woman became a second mother to Edith. Together they grew spiritually. Edith loved reading her Bible and was soon baptized. At night school, she shared Jesus with friends and teachers, who often looked to Edith for advice.

One night while fasting and praying in her bedroom, she received God's gift of the Holy Spirit and call to serve God full-time. God miraculously provided the registration fee, books, and bus fare to attend the Theological Institute, where she became one of my students. One day, Edith asked for an appointment with me. She shared her painful secrets. After a time of counseling and praying together, she forgave her mother. That November morning, chains of hate and bitterness broke.

I encouraged Edith to express her forgiveness to her mother. At this time, it had been four years since she even knew where her mother lived. While she was still trying to locate her, Edith received a letter from her mother, who turned out to be living in Concepcion, a port city on the Paraguay River about four hundred kilometers from Asuncion. Edith's sister Isabel, who was living in another city by now, also wanted to reconnect with their mother, so together the two sisters booked passage on a boat to Concepcion.

On December 23, the sisters located the shack in which their mother was living with a drunk boyfriend and her most recent children, ages seven, three, and one. They were dirty and used bad language. Their mother didn't recognize Edith and Isabel at first. They hugged her, weeping with joy.

Then Edith shared with her mother God's Christmas gift of His Son, explaining that Jesus could change her as He had changed Edith. Edith also told her mother that she loved her and forgave her for the abandonment and mistreatment as a child. They prayed together, and her mother accepted Jesus, the best Christmas present possible.

Edith and Isabel convinced their mother to move back to Asuncion, where they could help her. Gathering up the meager belongings in the tiny shack, they took a boat back to Asuncion, where they found a small house to rent. Once Isabel returned to her home, Edith took on the role of mother, setting rules on money management, sleeping habits, caring for the children, church attendance, and cleanliness. Gradually with daily prayer, God's Word, and patience, they saw positive change. Scars from years of sinful living remained, but Edith's mother continued to grow spiritually.

When Edith graduated from the Theological Institute, she was no longer timid or bitter as when she first attended but walked confidently and smiling across the platform to receive her diploma from my husband. She later became a schoolteacher. Over the years she was able to share God's love with countless children

Chapter Thirty-Four: Starting Again

who'd experienced similar traumas, and many accepted God's transforming gift of abundant life.

Throughout that first year in Paraguay, we continued to witness miracle after miracle, both at evangelistic tent campaigns and in the lives of students and youth. One twenty-one-year-old named Chongue was suffering from an advanced ulcer that had not responded to any treatment or diet. At a tent campaign, she received Christ as Savior, then went on to place her hands on her stomach and pray for healing as instructed by a guest evangelist from the United States, Tom Wagoner. She immediately felt God's power heal her and celebrated with a feast of foods she'd hadn't been able to eat for months.

Jose, a street vendor, had developed a badly infected foot, making it very painful to push his cart through the cobblestoned streets. After evangelist Roy Brewer prayed for him at a tent campaign, Jose caused a commotion stomping his foot and shouting, "God has healed my foot!"

One Saturday, a second-year student Antonio traveled to an isolated Guarani village where a smiling woman named Juana welcomed him. Earlier, God had impressed on Juana's heart that she should seek out an evangelical church to be healed of the cataracts that had been blinding her for two years. With her daughter as guide, she attended an AG church in Asuncion where Antonio served as treasurer. She was instantly healed, and her return home without any further need of a guide drew the attention of her entire village.

Since inviting her families and friends to travel to Asuncion wasn't practical, Juana had invited Antonio to come and share the gospel with her village. Speaking in Guarani, Antonio shared the plan of salvation. Almost the entire village raised their hands to accept Christ as Savior, and a new church was born.

Just one twenty-four hour window in October 1988 gives a snapshot of God's working in Paraguay. On Friday, 8 p.m., a Korean student, Daniel Ko, saved and discipled in Paraguay, called to tell us that he and his wife had been invited to organize an evangelistic outreach to Korean and Spanish youth in New York City. At 10 p.m., some of our students joined local Christian youth for a night vigil seeking God at a nearby church. At 2 a.m., two waiters heading home from their shift at a nearby restaurant were attracted by the singing. They entered the church, where the young people led them to Jesus. The following day, one waiter's mother and two teen sisters saw his positive change and accepted Christ.

That Saturday afternoon at 4 p.m., we held an appreciation fiesta for long and short-term ministry volunteers from different countries. The height of the fiesta was Bernard, who shared emotionally how a car accident had left him on crutches until God had transformed and healed him at a tent campaign these volunteers had helped make possible. Another student reflected that within a year nine of his immediate family had accepted Christ and twenty of his extended family were now serving the Lord. The student himself was pastoring a growing congregation of four hundred plus in attendance.

He concluded, "God gave to you. You gave to me. I am giving to others."

The twenty-four hour ended that evening at 8 p.m. with Bill sharing at a weekend youth conference in San Lorenzo. Over thirty teens heard the gospel for the first time, repeated the sinners' prayer, and left the building walking with Christ.

Chapter Thirty-Five

A Difficult Year

1989 was a difficult year for Bill and me and indeed for all of Paraguay. We had already been saddened by the loss of Bill's father not many months after arriving in Paraguay. Beebop, as all the grandkids and neighbor children called him, had suffered many years with heart disease. When saying goodbye at the airport, he'd taken Bill aside and told him lovingly, "Son, this is the last time I'll see you. Be faithful to God. Preach the Word. I'll be waiting for you inside the gates of pearl."

As was their custom, Bill's parents had attended the Wednesday evening church service. After the service, they'd stayed at the altar while Beebop led a young man to the Lord. They'd returned home, where Beebop ate his usual cookie with a glass of milk before lying down to sleep. Waking up early the next morning, Grandma slipped out to the kitchen to prepare breakfast. She returned to their bedroom to awaken Beebop to eat. That is when she discovered he was already enjoying heaven.

When he learned of Beebop's death, the young man Bill's father had led to Christ the previous evening pledged that he would take Beebop's place in serving God. We weren't able to fly home for the funeral, but in Beebop's honor, the Theological

Chapter Thirty-Five: A Difficult Year

Institute closed while students and faculty crammed into our little rented house to pray with us and sing about our heavenly home.

Then in February 1989, General Andrés Rodríguez led a military coup against the thirty-five-year reign of dictator Alfredo Stroessner. I was invited to speak that evening at a national women's retreat in a rural camp facility. The other women were staying overnight for the two-day event, but I left for home after the evening service was over.

It was close to midnight when I reached the main road leading from the Asuncion airport into the city. Scores of army tanks were heading into the city. I wondered what the occasion was since midnight was too late for a military parade. Maybe they were taking the tanks into the city to set up for a parade the next day.

Edging my way in between two tanks, I waved at the young soldiers as I drove along with them. I had turned off the main road toward our house when I heard what I thought were fireworks, a typical part of any celebration in Latin America. Was there a local holiday I didn't know about?

When I arrived home, Bill was very glad to see me. He immediately burst out, "Honey, do you have any idea what's going on? It's a military coup. Those aren't fireworks you're hearing but gunfire and grenades. President Stroessner has been overthrown, and all communication has been taken over by the military generals."

As foreign residents in Paraguay, we were registered with the U.S. embassy for events and security. Bill served as embassy liaison for our Assemblies of God missionary team. The embassy contacted my husband to advise all our American and other expat personnel to stay inside their residences. Throughout the night, my husband listened to the BBC news on short-wave radio while I called each team member, asking them to take precautions and keep calm, then praying together. How grateful I was to be safely home as others were caught in the crossfire of the military coup.

Eventually, the political situation calmed down. Stroessner fled into exile in Brazil. Rodriguez became the president, and a new constitution was voted in that allowed for free elections with a limit of only a single five-year presidential term that permitted no reelections, a reaction to Stroessner's thirty-five-year seizure of power that remains until this day.

But 1989 continued to be difficult. Bill was chairman of Paraguay's Assemblies of God missionary team. Most of his responsibilities were pleasant, and we constantly saw God intervening in response to searching, open hearts. But one after another, we had to confront and dismiss from ministry several colleagues due to misconduct. This broke our hearts and negatively affected national believers.

More devastating was a telephone call from one of our children confessing a deceptive lifestyle. There were tears on both ends as we went through the process of repentance, God's forgiveness, and restoration. Bill encouraged me to fly immediately back to the United States. He took over my classes while I caught the first flight I could. When I arrived in the United States, our child and I wept together as childhood/teen secrets bubbled over.

Afterwards, I turned to God, crying out with a broken heart. I needed to hear from Him. I opened the Bible and was stunned and grateful when my eyes fell on Isaiah 44:3: "I will pour my Spirit into your descendants and my blessing on your children." (NLT)

Chapter Thirty-Five: A Difficult Year

I knew God had heard me and would answer in His perfect timing. I wrote out the verse and put it on our refrigerator door, where it became my anchor for months. These difficult events devastated Bill and me. We'd always believed that our example as a Christian family was more important than our teaching. Now we felt total failures.

We shared our hurts with colleagues who prayed with us. We will always be grateful for the kind understanding and support we received from godly leaders during this traumatic year. We also realized we needed God's intervention in our personal lives. We'd heard about Link Care Center, a residential Christian counseling practice in California, from a college friend and pastor who served on its board. Bill flew to the United States, and we spent three weeks at Link. All three of our children joined us for family counselling. Intense reflection, encouragement, and sharing each morning along with manual work in the afternoons resulted in what I describe as a "bath in God's grace."

While still in the United States, we learned that Dad, his wife Christine, and their son David had arrived in Tulsa, Oklahoma, from India. We were able to route our flights through Tulsa to visit them before returning to Paraguay. David would soon be graduating from a private Christian high school in India and wanted to further his education in communication. He asked what college in the United States we would recommend. We suggested Evangel University, an Assemblies of God college in Springfield, Missouri.

David completed the application, and later Bill and I drove David to Evangel campus. When the admissions assistant heard the name David Groves, she expressed excitement. While she'd been reviewing the large folder of incoming freshmen applications, David's application had caught her attention. God had impressed on her that He had great plans for this young man from India.

She left us to speak to her boss. A short time later, the admissions director along with his assistant approached us. He turned to my younger brother. "David, we welcome you to Evangel. This lady has never spoken to me like this before. She is not emotional, so I believe her when she says God has shown her great plans for you. We'd like to give you an academic scholarship and provide on-campus work for you."

David eventually graduated from Evangel with a communications degree. He volunteered in media production in Brussels, Belgium, then accepted a position in the UK producing international Alpha courses, an interactive series that explores the basics of the Christian faith. He currently serves as program director of the popular UK Faith and Family TBN television station. As a family, we are all so proud of David!

Over the difficult months of 1989, Bill and I had discussed leaving public ministry. Now we experienced God's embrace of acceptance and recommissioning. We returned to Paraguay with grateful hearts, where we openly shared our journey with colleagues. As we did so, others realized that such counsel would help their own family challenges. Valuable lessons learned in this difficult year enriched our personal lives, family bonds, and future service.

Chapter Thirty-Six

Open-Heart Surgery

In 1990, I taught forty first-year students at the Theological Institute in Asuncion. We studied Joshua 7, which is the story of Israel's defeat at Ai and the hidden sin of Achan that was the cause of God allowing their defeat.

As the Holy Spirit searched hearts and applied the lesson of how God judges hidden sin, the atmosphere became tense. Cheating and copying homework assignments were accepted cultural habits in Paraguay. Many of our students had participated in such throughout grade school, high school, college, and even into their theological studies. Now they were uncomfortable as God's Word clearly revealed these practices as sin.

Some bowed their heads in remorse with tears dampening their desks. Spontaneously, students began to confess their cheating. One top student, Rose, asked, "How can I make things right with Professor Jim who taught Pentateuch last semester? I shared my answers with class-mates in his class."

The professor and his wife had moved to another city more than four hundred kilometers away. Other students admitted they too had cheated in that class and asked how they could contact him to ask forgiveness and have their final grades reduced. We had no cell phones or email access at that time, so there was no straightforward way to contact him.

Just then, we heard a hard knock on our classroom door. School rules prohibited interrupting classes except in emergencies, so it was with reluctance that I opened the door. I stared in disbelief. Standing in the doorway was Professor Jim. Astonished, the students rushed around him, tearfully confessing their wrongdoing. A sacred time of repentance and forgiveness brought spiritual healing.

During the remainder of their studies, I could trust these students to honestly prepare and present their own assignments. God's double-bladed surgeon's knife—His Word and His Spirit—had removed confessed sin during successful operations on these students' open hearts!

A highlight of 1990 was the inauguration of Noah's Ark, an ark-shaped building adjoining an Assemblies of God church in an outlying area of Asuncion densely populated with children. Just as we were about to cut the dedicatory ribbon and pray, God placed a bright double rainbow around the ark, for all to see. We jumped for joy, feeling God's gracious smile over this outreach. Thanks to Rich and Jenni DeMartino's vision and hard work, this novel children's center reached many area children and parents over the following years with God's love, drama, and fun.

Later that year, a large yellow-and-white striped tent housed a church plant in the town of Obligado for six months. We searched for a lot to build a permanent sanctuary, but we only had five thousand dollars donated for this project. One evening while Bill

Chapter Thirty-Six: Open Heart Surgery

was preaching, a businessman came into the tent offering a lot. It was in an ideal location, and he was asking a third of the going rate.

The next day, the pastor of this church plant, Francisco, introduced himself as the tent preacher to the city inspector and asked about zoning laws for the new lot. The inspector responded, "I don't want to talk about property. I want to talk about God. I planned to take my life this morning, and now you are here."

The two men prayed together, and that night the city inspector and his wife both accepted Christ at the tent campaign. The following day, the local priest was called to exorcise demons from three girls involved in Macumba, an Afro-Brazilian-type spirit worship. About three hundred people accompanied the priest, including the newly saved inspector and wife along with other government officials. The priest held a mass and tried to exorcise the demons, but nothing happened. He finally left. Then the crowd began calling out, "Call the tent preacher! He knows God."

Upon arriving at the large house courtyard where the crowd was gathered, Pastor Francisco demanded with supernatural authority, "In the Name of Jesus, come out of this house, Satan."

Immediately, the three girls emerged meekly, completely delivered from Satan's bondage. The crowd was amazed. Francisco explained that God's power saves, heals, and delivers when we submit to Him. Over two hundred-fifty people knelt on the ground, asking Jesus to be their Savior. They became the nucleus of another new church plant.

During this time period, I'd read an article of how God was powerfully using a drama called *Heaven's Gates and Hell's Flames* (commonly shortened to *Heaven's Gates*) that visualizes life after death. I felt strongly that this tool could bless Paraguay. Bill was more hesitant since we were already committed to many outreaches, but after we prayed together, he agreed. I researched the ministry, which was based in Canada, and invited the founder Rudy Krulik to launch this drama in Paraguay.

We prepared for six nightly presentations featuring a fifty-member all-Paraguayan cast. Students from the Theological Institute promoted and participated in the event. During that week, fifteen hundred people responded to the drama by accepting Christ, including entire families. One twenty-two-year-old soldier who accepted Christ was killed the following day while on military maneuvers along the Paraguay River. We are so thankful God allowed him a final opportunity to experience eternal life.

A layman from a local Roman Catholic church was impressed with the clear salvation message presented through drama. He asked permission to show the video we'd made of the performance in local parishes. When the director of programs for a major Paraguayan TV channel saw the drama, he asked to show the video nationwide free of charge. This was the first of scores of presentations throughout the country.

The drama was shown for six nights in the Paraguayan/Brazilian border city of Port Franco. Three hundred-fifty young people signed decision cards to follow Christ, including many drug addicts, dealers, and car thieves. These transformed youth were baptized in water and became part of a

Chapter Thirty-Six: Open Heart Surgery

new believers' class who now enjoyed serving their community instead of preying on it.

A wave of high-profile teen suicides swept Paraguay during the 1990s, the result of signing life contracts with Satan, Heartbroken, I embraced and prayed with parents of a beautiful twelve-year-old girl. Feeling trapped by evil, she'd found a gun and killed herself. How could I help? Since many thousands throughout the country had by now seen the drama in person or on a TV screen, I created a short video showing the seemingly innocent initial steps leading to these suicide tragedies reported daily in the news.

With approval by the *Heaven's Gates* ministry directors, this brief scene exposed spiritual warfare. Many youth who had manifested Satan's destructive power were delivered and set free to live productive, happy lives in submission to God.

One special joy serving overseas is the close bond with team members. Our dear colleagues Dr. Rodney and wife Lynn Hart had been associated with David Wilkerson in Teen Challenge's early years. In May 1992, Rodney motivated, coordinated, and helped finance the construction of the first evangelical chapel in Paraguay's national penitentiary, Tacumbu. Recognized for his success with drug addicts, Rodney was named Protestant chaplain for the facility.

When the chapel was completed, prison officials, former inmates being discipled in Paraguay's Teen Challenge rehabilitation center, present inmates, and friends were invited to the inauguration. Rodney's wife and their three small children accompanied Rodney to the event. When they arrived, Rodney with his chaplain's identification was immediately admitted. But Lynn and the children had to stand in line with hundreds of family members waiting to see prisoners during this weekly visitation day.

Lynn had dressed in a modest, full pant-skirt and blouse. But when she and the children finally reached the large iron gates, a guard curtly advised, "Women can't enter the prison wearing pants."

This was a strict prison rule at that time. Lynn tried to explain that what she was wearing was actually a divided skirt, but the guard wouldn't budge. Lynn said, "Look, my husband is the prison chaplain, and I've come a long way with my children to accompany him for the inauguration of the new prison chapel. What are my options?"

The guard just shrugged. "There's a booth near the main entrance where drinks and candy are sold. Maybe you can rent a skirt there."

Rather than return home, Lynn bravely approached the booth. The salesclerk pointed to bright skirts hanging from a nail. "Yes, we have two styles."

The skirts were short and of a brightly-colored psychedelic pattern, not a style Lynn would ever choose. But she bought one and slipped it over her own divided pant-skirt. Her children giggled at the sight as they helped her slide off her original attire. Once again, they lined up in the brutally hot sun. This time the guard waved them through.

As Lynn and her children walked through the filthy, smelly prison corridors crowded with over eighteen hundred angry prisoners crammed into a space designed for six hundred, she was challenged by their desperation. She was also perturbed by the way they stared at her short skirt and bare legs, wishing she could hold up a sign declaring, "This is not my skirt!"

When they finally arrived at the packed chapel, the inauguration ceremony was in progress. Rodney took in his wife's changed appearance with a confused expression. When she quietly whispered the reason for her delay and change of clothes, Rodney hugged her, saying, "Honey, I'm proud of you!"

He proceeded to introduce her to visiting dignitaries. The event became an exciting celebration as Rodney, Lynn, government officials, along with former drug addicts, traffickers, and criminals raised hearts and hands in grateful thanks to God for His transforming power. Lynn felt overjoyed that through her husband's testimony and ministry so many hopeless prisoners were now followers of Jesus Christ. Somehow a rented skirt didn't seem so important anymore!

Chapter Thirty-Seven

Running in High Heels

One day around noon, I was returning home from teaching when I decided to stop at a German market to purchase some of their delicious fresh-baked bread. I parked and was locking a borrowed jeep I was driving when a teenager approached me.

My first thought was that he either knew me or needed help. But when he got close, he violently snatched my purse containing important documents, cash, and glasses, as well as my ring of car/house keys with which I was locking the car. He nearly pulled my finger off. Turning, he ran. Without hesitating, I ran after him in my high heels, screaming, "Not my documents!"

A uniformed armed guard saw me running but couldn't leave his post. As I ran up a hill, a man waiting at the nearby bus stop saw my predicament and began running with me. I found out later that he was an optician who just three months earlier had donated his kidney to his daughter, who was on dialysis, so he wasn't supposed to be running. But he insisted on helping me find this thief.

"We want Asuncion's streets to be safe," he explained. "The police can't do everything."

Chapter Thirty-Seven: Running in High Heels

As we ran up the cobble-stoned street, the thief turned a corner and disappeared from sight. Chasing him around the corner, we asked pedestrians and residents if they had seen a teenager with a striped shirt running.

"Yes," they responded, "but we didn't know why he was running."

Finally, we asked some electricians up on telephone poles if they'd seen a teen running past them. When they answered in the negative, we concluded the thief must be hiding within this two-block area. The optician searched one side of the road while I checked bushes, trees, patios, and house entrances on the other side. The optician jumped up on a brick fence surrounding an empty lot. He soon saw a striped shirt in the tall weeds. Jumping down into the lot, he wrestled the thief to the ground. Two nearby construction workers helped haul the teen into the street.

"I have him!" the optician shouted to me.

I immediately identified the young man by his striped shirt, but he strongly denied he was the thief. Neighbors had by now gathered to see the drama. They advised me to report the theft to the police. When a passing car slowed, I asked the driver if he could take me to the closest police station. He kindly agreed.

Before we got there, we found two policemen walking toward the scene, having already received a call from a witness. They jumped into the car. On arrival, the police asked the teen a series of questions, handcuffed him, and found my cash stuffed in his pockets.

"Where are the lady's documents, keys, purse, and other belongings?" the policemen demanded. The teen finally took us to a car port. I crawled under a parked car to retrieve my valuable documents. Then he led us to my keys and glasses, which had been tossed into the high weeds surrounding a telephone pole.

I sincerely thanked the optician, who had been God's angel to help a foreigner in need. Retrieving my vehicle, I drove my handcuffed assailant and the two policemen to the police station. There I gave my statement while the police chief wrote it down by hand, which took at least two hours. Many policemen stopped by, fascinated to hear this foreign woman's story. I asked the police chief for the teen's name so I could later visit and pray with him.

When he finished taking my report, the police chief looked into my eyes. "Lady, God protected you! This is a miracle that never happens. The thief wasn't armed, and you weren't injured. You have all your stolen belongings, and the criminal is in custody. Even your glasses are unbroken."

"Sir, God's angels protected me because I am His child," I responded.

He agreed, adding that his wife was an evangelical. I then asked permission to speak with the teen. Through the bars of the holding cell, I quickly told him that God loved him and had a much better plan for His life. Briefly, I shared God's plan of salvation and prayed with him, promising to return later and bring him a Bible.

I arrived home thankful but exhausted from the trauma and heat. I flopped onto our couch. Bill arrived sometime later and excitedly shared, "Honey, I had the most wonderful time sharing with more than seventy employees at Camagro, a car parts business. During their lunch break, many accepted Christ as Savior."

Chapter Thirty-Seven: Running in High Heels

"Honey, you shared Jesus in a nice commercial property," I responded teasingly. "I just shared Jesus in a steaming-hot jail!"

That night when I arrived at the Theological Institute campus to teach a class, I found that the faculty and students had all heard about my encounter. They joined in advising strongly, "Sister Hilda, this is a miracle, and we are proud of you. But don't ever run after a thief again!"

I went back to take the teen a Bible, but he'd already been moved. Though I looked for him at several different prisons under the direction of the police, I was sadly unable to find him and keep my promise. I was, however, able to return to the police station with cookies, recorded Christian music, and Bible portions for the policemen who had been so kind to me, a foreigner.

During this same time period, Bill and I lost our last living parent—my father. Knowing he wasn't doing well, Pauline and I traveled to Bangalore in January 1994 to visit him for two weeks. He was now in his eighties and visibly frail, but we celebrated his birthday on January 30th with a special meal of curry and rice. David also came from Evangel College in Springfield, where he was studying.

While we were there, Christine contacted a doctor to check on Dad. The doctor arrived on his motorbike, carrying a satchel. He was quite young, and I watched from the open bedroom door as he examined Dad. I will never forget the precious scene that followed when the doctor asked Dad to pray for him. Laying his weak, trembling hand on the young doctor's arm, Dad prayed, the patient now blessing the doctor!

Many Muslims, Buddhists, and Christians visited Dad during our visit. Dad prayed with each one, including God's plan of salvation in each prayer. I asked local missionaries about these visitors. Dad wasn't a social person, so I knew they weren't all personal friends. The missionaries responded that these people had heard Dad was dying and wanted to honor him as a holy man of God.

Before we left, Dad said to my sister and me, "Pauline and Hilda, my address will soon be Glory. Although my body is closing down, inside my spirit is dancing!"

Sure enough, just two weeks after Pauline and I finished our visit on February 20, 1994, Dad slipped into God's presence. We were so thankful we'd been able to say our goodbyes in person. Representatives from the AG missionary body, a pastor from Calcutta, and a local Indian pastor all spoke at his funeral. The pastor from Calcutta, who'd known my father's ministry well over the decades, commented that he didn't know of any convert whom the Groves had discipled who'd later drifted away from faith, a wonderful testimony to my father's ministry.

After his death, Christine continued serving God through mission trips. After David graduated from college and moved to England, she joined him there, where they both presently live.

Chapter Thirty-Eight

Radical Contrasts, Different Perspectives

I was jolted one weekend as I witnessed two radical contrasts that reflected much of the Paraguayan culture in which we served. A middle class didn't seem to exist. Bill and I were living short-term in a house while the tenants, missionary colleagues of ours, were on furlough in the United States. Early in the week, we heard construction noise and saw constant activity in an elegant mansion across from our house as these wealthy neighbors prepared for their daughter's wedding reception.

Workers laid wooden planks over manicured lawns to facilitate dancing. Round mirror-topped tables reflected shiny silver coffee and tea sets. Life-size sculptures of cows, chickens, and pigs indicated the meats to be served. Imported flowers covered stately columns at the mansion's entrance. On Friday and Saturday, scores of vehicles delivered supplies, food, and drinks.

On Saturday evening, I watched from our upstairs window as expensive cars parked in front of our house and on adjoining streets where many residences were just ramshackle shacks. Many guests were chauffeured, and their attire reflected latest fashion designs. Political leaders arrived under police escort. A professional band blasted loud music throughout the neighborhood until 3 a.m. The Sunday national newspaper described the event with photos, but I saw no real joy on the faces of those attending.

What a contrast to an indigenous Guarani woman named Eyda who faithfully helped clean our house and do food preparation twice weekly. Eyda sang as she worked. One Saturday, she begged me to visit her elderly parents in their humble home outside the city so that I could pray for them. After she finished work, I drove her home. Parking the vehicle at the foot of a dirt trail, we climbed up a steep incline to the tiny house where Eyda lived with her two children. Her husband had long since abandoned the family.

Her parents lived in a similar shack nearby cobbled together from bricks, pieces of wood, and tin, the window spaces covered with burlap sacking. I prayed for them with Eyda translating my Spanish into their Guarani language. She then proudly introduced her precious children and showed me her cow, chickens, plants, and vegetable garden.

Eyda had already gathered gifts for my husband and me—cassava tubers, eggs, beans, cilantro, cabbage, and some beautiful house plants. She placed one large potted plant on her head and grabbed bags of produce in each hand as she sedately walked back down the trail to my parked vehicle. Overwhelmed by her generosity, I said, "Eyda, you have blessed me so much today and every time you come to our home. May I bless you also?"

I tried to hand her some money, but tears welled up in her eyes as she refused. "Sister Hilda. I'm so happy to give you what I have because I love you. When I was in such need, you helped me."

Chapter Thirty-Eight: Radical Contrasts, Different Perspectives

She was referencing a politically powerful neighbor who had approached Eyda with a seemingly legal document, stating that her family's property actually belonged to him and threatening eviction. Eyda had produced the original legitimate deed that showed the property had been purchased by her family several generations prior. Bill and I had directed Eyda to a Christian lawyer who was a member of a large AG church in Asuncion. He'd helped her fight her legal battle, and the case had been settled in favor of Eyda and her family.

As Bill and I unloaded these wonderful gifts from our car, we once again concluded that money doesn't buy happiness. God blesses a generous heart. Yes, we've observed some happy rich Paraguayans who were followers of Jesus and generously gave to serve the needy, that Christian lawyer being one example. But we'd also witnessed thousands of Paraguayans considered poor but rich in faith and generously serving others just as the apostle Paul once praised the Macedonian church for giving joyfully out of their own extreme poverty (2 Corinthians 8:1-5).

On a later occasion, I experienced two very different but accurate perspectives of my heavenly Father. Looking through special eclipse shades into a cloudless sky from our balcony in Asuncion, Bill and I with other friends witnessed what was being described as nature's phenomenon of the century. Scientists and observers from around the world filled every hotel room since Paraguay was considered one of the best locations to see the complete solar eclipse. At 8.30 a.m. on November 3, 1994, we traced the moon as it slowly covered the sun, engulfing the capital in complete darkness for 3 ½ minutes. Roosters crowed, dogs barked, and animals looked for their night shelter.

As we observed the beauty of the sun's radiance from behind the moon, we recognized God's miraculous precision controlling the course of heavenly bodies. We echoed David's comments in Psalms.

> The heavens declare the glory of God: the skies proclaim the work of His hands. (Psalm 19:1 NIV)

What a contrast of perspective to our Bible Institute administrator's cute five-year-old son Joshua, who walked into Bill's office pointing to his brand-new black, shiny shoes. Joshua had been praying for new shoes for a long time. His participation in an end-of-school drama made his prayer more urgent. When Bill complimented his little friend on his new acquisition, Joshua proudly lifted his trouser legs and responded, "The Lord is my shepherd, I shall not want" (Psalm 23:1 KJV).

In a single week I'd been awed by God's majestic light show in His immense universe. At the same time, Joshua reminded me that our mighty, infinite God who juggles the entire universe with perfect precision listens and responds to a kindergarten child's practical requests.

Another very different contrast can be summarized from a Paraguayan newspaper report in 1993. One of our Theological Institute students, Carlos, had come to Christ through a youth event where Bill had preached. He'd met his sweetheart Marizza, a first-grade teacher and committed follower of Jesus, while they

Chapter Thirty-Eight: Radical Contrasts, Different Perspectives

were both working at a Christian school. After a two-year courtship, they were scheduled to be married in just three days.

Staunch Catholics, Marizza's parents had been furious when she accepted Christ and left their church to attend an evangelical church. They were even more furious over her marrying a Theological Institute student. Three days before the wedding, Marizza's father and some other relatives made a surprise visit to Marizza's house. They invited her and Carlos to go with them for a pre-wedding celebration at the home of extended family in another town. They agreed. Carlos rode in her father's car while Marizza rode in an uncle's vehicle. Everyone seemed happy.

But instead of driving to the other town, Marizza's father drove Carlos out to a remote rural area. Pulling a gun, he abruptly stopped the car and ordered Carlos to get out. Then he sped off. When Carlos finally made his way home, he discovered that the uncle had kidnapped Marriza at her parents' behest to prevent her marrying a non-Catholic.

Carlos was determined to rescue his beloved. Since the Paraguayan constitution guaranteed freedom of religion, he took legal action. A judge ordered a search for Marizza, and the press published the story. For five days, Marizza was locked under guard in a room at her grandmother's house. But her father, uncle, cousins, and other relatives became increasingly nervous over the escalating press coverage and police search. To avoid prosecution, they finally decided to release their captive.

Marizza was handed over to the police, who drove her to Carlos's home. The couple immediately set a new date for their marriage. Marizza's family didn't attend, but Carlos's family and many fellow Theological Institute students and members of their church cheered as this young Christian couple pledged their union.

The newlyweds chose to restore relationships by expressing their love to Marizza's family. But their story was an example of continued religious persecution and prejudice that exists in Paraguay, vestiges of the centuries when the Catholic church was the only legal state church of Paraguay and controlled every aspect of society from marriages, births, education, even burials.

Contrast this with another major Paraguayan press report in July 1994 that told of tens of thousands of evangelical Christians and even many Catholics marching through the streets of Asuncion with banners proclaiming the gospel, followed by a public outdoors worship service. The event was part of a *Marcha Para Jesus* (March for Jesus) taking place simultaneously in many countries, all across Latin America.

A top Paraguayan newspaper headlined the story as *Una Manifestación Diferente* (A Different Manifestation) because the last five years of Paraguay's wobbly transition from a thirty-five-year repressive dictatorship to democracy had included many violent protests and angry marches.

In contrast, here were tens of thousands of Christians peacefully marching, lifting Jesus high in songs, banners, and literature. Across Latin America alone, the *Marcha Para Jesus* included several million participants in the various city marches, an indication of how much God's kingdom and the evangelical church had grown in Latin America, especially since Vatican 2.

The Asuncion march culminated with prayer for government leaders and the country's spiritual healing. In the news coverage, the Asuncion police chief was quoted as saying, "Rather than protest, you sang. Rather than ridicule, you prayed for our police force. This is our first experience of a positive public manifestation of God's love."

Chapter Thirty-Nine

Hora Feliz

4 p.m. on Thursdays was *Hora Feliz,* or Happy Hour, for Bill and me. This came about as we moved into a remodeled home in a lower-income neighborhood in Asuncion. Our next-door neighbor approached me. "I'm Dona Benita. You are an evangelical, right?"

"Yes, we love and serve Jesus," I replied.

"Then would you teach me to pray?" she asked.

I was overjoyed at the request. "Of course, I will be most happy. Maybe other neighbors would like to join us."

That became the beginning of a weekly women's Bible study and prayer time in our home. I also saw many children playing on our cobble-stoned street, so at our next meeting I asked the neighborhood women if I could hold a teaching time in our outdoor patio for the children that would include learning English, Bible stories, puppets, singing, and a snack. They were happy for any learning opportunity for their children, especially since a knowledge of English was advantageous for school and future careers.

Thus was born our Thursday afternoon *Hora Feliz*, or Happy Hour. I invited each family on our street with a printed invitation.

Chapter Thirty-Nine: Hora Feliz

A missionary colleague who specialized in children's outreaches gave us a puppet stage with several puppets. After an English lesson, we sang gospel choruses, taught brief Bible stories, prayed, and memorized scriptures. Many mothers accompanied their children, also hearing the gospel.

Though I loved teaching in the Theological Institute and other contexts, this weekly event became the highlight of my week. Another missionary colleague and students from the Theological Institute helped. At least sixty children accepted Jesus along with some of the mothers. It was a pleasure to walk around the neighborhood around mealtimes and hear children as well as parents singing the prayer of thanks we always sang together before serving the Happy Hour snack.

We continued to be blessed by the stories of God's working in our students. One evening student named Fanny shared with me in 1995 that she needed a good job as she was the breadwinner for her mother and six siblings. We prayed together in the school patio, asking God for a miracle. The following week, Fanny was selected from sixty applicants to work in a large real estate management company.

On her first day, Fanny arrived early at her desk, opened her Bible, and quietly prayed, *Thank you, Jesus, for this job. May I bless this company by my work and attitude.*

As she prayed, another employee entered. The young woman was surprised and pleased to see the new employee praying with an open Bible. She introduced herself as a believer and asked, "If I come early, would you like to have devotions together before work hours?"

Fanny happily agreed. Each day the two young women read a Scripture passage and prayed. One morning the company owner entered just as Fanny was praying, "Lord, please bless and prosper this company and leadership. Help me learn quickly and be an asset to employees and bosses."

The owner was stunned. She told the two young women, "I have heard employees complain, lose tempers, and curse me. But I have never heard anyone pray for me and the company. Thank you!"

Fanny was soon praying each workday with all the employees, sharing a fifteen-minute weekly Bible study, and writing Bible devotionals to be included in promotional materials the company circulated to Paraguayan businesses. She shared with me, "Sister Hilda, we prayed I would find just one good job. Now I'm a secretary, a pray-er, a preacher, a counsellor, and a writer!"

Together we thanked God for answering prayer.

This same year, a short-term missions team from the United States helped construct a needed addition to our growing Theological Institute. They also donated three hundred reading glasses. After fitting a student named Jorge with glasses, team members asked if he had a need for which they could pray. Jorge shared his heavy heart. His mother had abandoned him when he was six. He'd never received word from or about her. Now at twenty years old, he longed to contact her.

The team members earnestly prayed with Jorge. The very next day, his mother called an Asuncion police station looking for her

Chapter Thirty-Nine: Hora Feliz

son. The call came all the way from Puerto Rico, where she was now living. Jorge was able to use his church's telephone to talk with his mother. That Christmas, their family reunited in Puerto Rico.

Each month Bill had to cash donations in U.S. currency into our Paraguayan currency, called *guarani* after the country's majority population group, to cover the expenses of the Theological Institute and other ministries. For security reasons, Bill took a local taxi service to the money exchange, had the driver wait, then came back in the same taxi.

On one return trip, the taxi driver began sharing personal needs and realized he needed divine help. Bill explained how to receive God's gift of eternal life. When they arrived back at the Theological Institute, the two men stayed in the taxi praying as the taxi driver gave his life's steering wheel to Jesus. Bill found a Bible for the taxi driver to take with him. The next day, we heard the tragic news that this taxi driver had been held up, robbed, and murdered. We were so thankful that he'd met Jesus the day before and God had welcomed him into His divine presence.

In 1996, we traveled back to the U.S. for furlough. Later that year, God took Bill's sweet mother to her eternal home. Our son Phil wrote a letter to his grandmother that he read at her memorial service:

Dear Grandma: Greetings from all your grandchildren Debbie, Tim, Mark, Jeffrey, Ruth, Cheryl and myself. We know you are smiling more than you have in a long time. You are now in the presence of Jesus and your best

> *friend on earth and now in heaven, Beebop [Grandpa]. If we were to look in the dictionary for the definition of servant, your photo would appear... As youngsters, trips to your house meant the best cookies, chicken-noodle soup, pepperoni balls, and pizzelles. As we grew older, trips to your house meant a safe haven where we always felt your love and servant attitude... I'm not alone with stories like this about you. We miss you a lot, but what you have taught us lives on.*

During this furlough, I received a sad letter from our neighbor Dona Benita concerning ten-year old Luis, one of the children who attended our Happy Hour. He came straight from soccer practice, so his sweaty clothes, face, and hair always contrasted other children's freshly brushed hair and clean clothes. But he loved to learn Bible verses and sing gospel songs, and he had accepted Jesus as Savior. Her note read:

> *I have sad news, Sister Hilda. Our whole street is grieving over Luis. Because the bus broke down, his return home was delayed. His impatient father lost his temper and hung Luis from their patio tree where he died.*

Heart-broken, I thanked God that Luis had experienced God's forgiveness before his brutal death. God rescued Luis from further abuse of a dysfunctional family and welcomed him into His eternal presence.

When we arrived back in Asuncion for another term of service, children emerged from hiding behind bushes and trees with big signs welcoming us home. With hugs and smiles, they asked when we could once again celebrate Happy Hour. Two older girls who were part of that group eventually moved and started their own Happy Hour in their new neighborhood. We loved seeing these transformed young ladies in action.

Paraguayan Children in Happy Hour.

Chapter Forty

What's Heaven Like?

A mechanic, Chino serviced several vehicles belonging to the Assemblies of God national church that transported tents for gospel campaigns as well as construction materials to build new churches in different parts of the country. Chino, his wife Techi, and their two children had always lived in cramped quarters, so they were excited when they were asked to house-sit a spacious mansion with a swimming pool while the owners travelled.

Entering the elegant vestibule, three-year-old Alex knelt and spontaneously thanked Jesus for such a beautiful mansion in which to live. That first Saturday, the family held a fiesta for relatives and friends. Children ran in and out of the house while mothers prepared food in the kitchen and the men cooked chicken and sausages on the outside barbeque.

Even at the age of three, Alex had a heart that was sensitive to God. The previous week while "helping" his mechanic dad repair trucks, he'd repeatedly asked questions about heaven. Chino had done his best to answer Alex's questions, and as they worked together, they'd sung gospel songs about heaven.

Chapter Forty: What's Heaven Like?

Suddenly, Techi's voice cut into the happy fiesta chatter. "Where's Alex?"

Everyone began searching. Rushing towards the swimming pool, Chino saw a dead bird floating on the water. As he got closer, he saw Alex at the bottom of the pool. He'd apparently jumped into the water to rescue the bird but couldn't swim.

Grabbing Alex out of the water, Chino immediately realized he'd already gone to heaven. But he raced with his son to a private Christian hospital, where he called us. Bill rushed to the emergency room. But neither medical expertise nor prayer brought Alex back. Chino cried out in anguish, "God, You lent Alex to us for three wonderful years. We give him back to You!"

Bill and I were amazed at Chino's attitude of thanksgiving rather than blaming God. The family requested that Bill speak at the funeral. Alex was to be buried in the family mausoleum. A large crowd filled the cemetery. Bill found an elevated mausoleum step on which to stand. We were all conscious of God's presence as Bill's loud, clear voice shared the scriptural truth of resurrection. Concluding, Bill gave public opportunity to accept God's gift of eternal life. Countless people in the crowd raised their hands to accept Jesus.

During all of this, I noticed a strange quietness with no dogs barking. Low, black, ominous clouds filled the sky. Then the clouds opened up. It was as though God had given us a quiet, still window to hear a word from heaven before a huge tropical storm pelted the area. We had to wait several hours in our vehicle before the flood waters receded from the cobble-stoned streets enough to drive home. We continued to wonder why God had chosen to allow the death of this precious child, but a loud and clear "Thank You!" burst from our hearts and lips to the One who does all things well.

Sometime later, I was invited to speak at our annual Paraguayan national retreat for the wives of AG pastors. During the event, I heard painful, heart-breaking cries. Investigating, I witnessed the anguish of a pastor's wife as she tried to calm her two-year-old son Samuelito, who had been born with his intestines outside of his frail little body. Medical specialists had already operated on him four times, but his condition continued to deteriorate.

My heart broke for this young pastor's family. When I returned to Asuncion, I shared the need of Pastor Osvaldo, Maria Celena, and their son Samuelito with dear friends Larry and Dee McGee, who were in Paraguay teaching some post-grad Christian ministry courses. Dee spoke up. "Hilda, I'm sure there are people and organizations who can help. When we return to the U.S., let me see what I can do."

After much researching and hard work, Dee wrote me with good news. An American Christian businessman had offered to pay eight thousand dollars toward medical expenses. A surgeon volunteered his expertise for the surgery. A local doctor donated his services during the child's surgery and follow-up treatment. Ronald MacDonald Charities, which supports the families of sick children, offered to house mother and child during their stay.

Meanwhile from Paraguay, I was able to arrange free air flights from American Airlines and medical visas from the U.S. embassy. St. John's Hospital in Springfield, MO, agreed to provide hospital care for all Samuelito's needs for the eight thousand dollars available.

Chapter Forty: What's Heaven Like?

We praised God for providing these amazing resources. But a huge obstacle remained. The American doctors needed Samuelito's Paraguayan medical records to evaluate his needs. Maria Celina repeatedly requested her son's medical file from the local children's hospital and his doctors. But she kept being put off with promises of *mañana* (tomorrow). Days turned to weeks and weeks to months while Samuelito grew weaker.

At a women's meeting in a missionary colleague's home, I requested prayer for this urgent need. We prayed as fervently as though Samuelito was our own son. When I arrived back home, Bill told me, "Maria Celina has been trying to talk to you."

She had walked several miles to the nearest telephone since the small town where her husband pastored didn't have one. When we finally connected on the phone, I heard her excitement. "The doctor received a new computer program to translate Spanish records to English. He has promised to release the medical records tomorrow!"

This was an answer to prayer. Early the next morning, Maria Celina received his large file. Finally, a date was set to fly to the United States. Bags, passports, and documents in hand, Maria Celena and Samuelito were seen off at the airport by a large group of family, neighbors, and friends. Maria Celina was scared, never having travelled by airplane. Her husband Osvaldo was worried to be sending his wife and sick son off alone. I reassured them, rehearsing the series of miracles and evidence of God's care that had brought this precious little family to this point.

Just as I was speaking, a woman edged her way into the group. "Sister Hilda. You don't know me, but I know you. Are you travelling to Miami? If so, we are on the same flight."

"No, I'm not," I responded. "I'm here to see this pastor's wife and her sick son off to a hospital in the United States.

I quickly explained the situation, then went on, "My dear sister, I believe that you are an angel sent from God to help Maria Celina and Samuelito on their first air flight."

"Of course, of course! Certainly, I will help them!" she agreed fervently. We all held hands, committing the travelers to our faithful heavenly Father. After many tears and hugs, Maria Celina and Samuelito boarded the flight with their protecting angel.

The flight to Miami had a layover in Sao Paulo. As Maria Celina struggled with a heavy bag and her crying son, another observant passenger went to an airport store and bought a carry-on with wheels and drinkable yogurt for mother and son. Maria Celena was stunned by this generous gift, especially since the other passenger couldn't have known that yogurt was the only drink her son could tolerate.

When they reached Miami, a U.S. immigration officer escorted mother and child to an inspection room. She questioned the medical record since Samuelito didn't seem ill to her. Then Maria Celena laid her son on a chair to change his diapers. Seeing his exposed intestines, the officer turned pale and quickly escorted them through Immigration, where they were welcomed to the United States.

Chapter Forty: What's Heaven Like?

Our daughter and several others welcomed Maria Celina and her son at the Springfield airport. This included Becky Powers, who had lived in Paraguay with her missionary parents. She contacted the local press to ask if they'd be interested in this inspiring story of generosity by Springfield citizens. TV cameras and reporters were at the airport to document the story. When it aired on various media outlets, people began bringing food, diapers, toiletries, and other items to Ronald McDonald House for Maria Celina and Samuelito.

Maria Celina spoke no English, but a Spanish-major college intern was assigned to chauffeur and translate during medical appointments. Daily, the media covered Samuelito's medical journey. Nurses, doctors, new friends, and church members expressed concern in many practical ways. Sunday School classes and other groups invited Maria Celina to share her story. School children raised funds to help cover expenses. A kindergartener raised seventy dollars outside of a Walmart store.

About three months after a successful surgery, Samuelito was given medical clearance to return to Paraguay. Together with family and neighborhood families, I joined a welcome home celebration at the Asuncion airport. That scene is indelibly etched in my memory. Maria Celina held a now healthy toddler dressed in new clothes and embracing his own soccer ball. When Samuelito saw his father, he squirmed out of his mother's arms and ran into Osvaldo's embrace.

Once home, Maria Celina opened an envelope containing monetary gifts from many Springfield residents. As she and her husband Osvaldo counted the money, they realized there was enough to pay for all the bills they'd accrued in Paraguay from the previous unsuccessful surgeries. They had experienced a true modern-day miracle, and thanks to God's healing care, compassionate friends and organizations, and generous professionals, a happy, healthy little boy was now reunited with his family.

Samuelito's First Smile.

Chapter Forty-One

A Walking Miracle

In 1998, we received word that my sister Pauline was dying from stage-four bone cancer. Bill offered to teach my classes, and I immediately booked a flight to Kalispell, Montana, the closest airport to their home in the scenic lakeside town of Bigfork.

Just three years older, Pauline had been a second mother to me, especially when our parents served on the other side of the world. She'd comforted me when I was missing my own mother. We'd moved to the U.S. together and attended Bible college together. Even after we were both married and ministry moved us thousands of miles apart, we kept in touch at every opportunity, laughing, crying, sharing sister secrets together. I'd been with Pauline and Halden when Jesus welcomed their six-year-old son David to his heavenly home.

Now my dear sister was facing another crisis. Doctors gave her no chance of survival. Family and friends had gathered at the hospital to say goodbye. But God's plan on this earth for Pauline was not yet finished. She later shared what was happening as to all appearances she lay unconscious in her hospital bed.

Pauline saw what seemed to be a merry-go-round, but instead of horses or other cute animals, the creatures revolving around the merry-go-round looked like fierce, evil monsters in attack mode. Standing around her bed, her family actually heard her saying "No! No! No!" to each creature as it spun past her. But one creature was covered in a pristine-white cloth. Pauline couldn't see what lay under the drapery, but she somehow knew that it was divine. In a clear voice, she said, "Yes!"

Immediately the figure was uncovered, and Pauline saw a beautiful eagle. She mounted its back, and together they soared into heaven. From her high vantage point, she could see her body on the hospital bed. Then the eagle turned and descended. Pauline suddenly found herself back in her body and conscious. Though she faced a long journey of prayer, chemotherapy, bone marrow transplants, and much care, she was alive.

When I arrived at the Curtiss home, I found my sister skeletally thin but with a strong spirit that praised the Lord. It was my honor to care for her over the next seven weeks so that Halden could continue carrying out his ministerial responsibilities. Daily, we wondered if Pauline would survive the morning. Her eyes were sunken, and she couldn't get up out of bed or keep more than small amounts of food down.

Expressions of love from the community overwhelmed us. Two local congregations made lists of those wanting to clean the house and bring food Pauline could eat. Food, flowers, telephone calls, personal visits, including children, filled each day. Though I didn't feel she wasn't strong enough, she invited friends over from near and far. Each left blessed and encouraged.

Stefan von Trapp, son of Werner von Trapp of the Trapp Family Singers (renamed Kurt in the movie *Sound of Music*), lived nearby with his wife Annie and four children Sofia, Melanie, Amanda, and Justin. The family attended the church Pauline and Halden pastored and had all inherited the von Trapp gift of song. One day they brought by fresh vegetables and flowers from their garden. As Pauline lay on the couch, they harmonized their melodic voices singing the farewell clock song from *Sound of Music*. When they were older, the four children formed a singing group called The Von Trapps, and their singing gifts have since taken them around the world.

During this time, Pauline experienced another supernatural visitation. She saw a large ship sailing towards her on peaceful blue water. *Healing in His Wings* was written clearly on each sail. As the ship docked, she saw that it was filled with happy people singing and praising God. Circular stairs led up to the ship's deck where the captain, smartly dressed in a white uniform, asked, "Pauline, are you ready to join us?"

As Pauline hesitated, the captain continued, "Wait here, and I'll return for your answer."

The captain left. Pauline thought of her family. She wanted to see her daughter married and her grandchildren grow up. Eventually, the captain returned and asked, "Are you ready?"

"I want to go," Pauline replied. "But I'm not ready to leave my family."

"That's fine." The captain pointed to the horizon. "Just remember, it's just the other side!"

Pauline saw this same vision three times. When she described it to her children, they insisted, "Mom, please don't board the ship when it docks next time!"

Each morning while I was there, Pauline and I enjoyed a devotional time together. We read God's Word. We expressed our confused thoughts and desires in prayer. We pondered Pauline's divine visitations, comforted by the knowledge that she was safe and peaceful in God's divine healing hands.

We drove to the hospital for Pauline's chemotherapy. The doctors and nurses always welcomed her gladly as her positive spirit uplifted the other patients receiving treatment. The chemo and other medications took their toll, leaving her nauseated and weak. She'd lost her hair and had to wear a wig.

But despite the doctors' dismal prognosis, Pauline began to improve as God's healing power touched her frail body. Once the Theological Institute classes finished in Asuncion, Bill joined us in Montana. By the time we left to fly back to Paraguay, Pauline was out of bed and taking a few wobbly steps.

"We will see you again healthy!" Bill assured my sister.

This seemed impossible. But once again we witnessed that impossible is not in God's vocabulary. To the doctors' astonishment, Pauline's cancer went into complete remission. She remains healthy and strong today though she struggles with some neuropathy from the high doses of chemotherapy. Her cancer doctor has since recommended many of his cancer patients to contact Pauline for encouragement and prayer. Her difficult journey through cancer became a great blessing to many people. I'm so grateful for a funny, faithful, fruitful, fabulous sister who is truly a walking miracle!

Chapter Forty-Two

Thieves!

One morning after our return to Paraguay, I had gone for an early walk with my next-door neighbor Benita in a nearby park, something we often did before the heat grew too uncomfortable to be outdoors. It was about 7 a.m. when I arrived back home. Just as I stepped through the front door, I saw men dashing out the back French doors that led to the patio. Backing out, I ran down our steps and over to Benita's adjoining house, calling out in Spanish, "Help! Help! Thieves!"

I saw a young man passing by on the street and asked him if he would go into my house with Benita and me, thinking that a male escort might be some protection if there were thieves still inside. He refused and quickly walked away, so instead I went into Benita's house and used her phone to call Bill, who had already gone to teach at the Theological Institute.

When I went back outside, a large muscular Brazilian man who lived on the other side of our house had emerged into the street. We hadn't ever met the owner of that house, which was a large property connected to a night club. But this man had rented a room there some months before, and we often saw him coming and going at odd hours of the day and night in different cars and with different women.

Coming over, he said, "I heard someone call for help. I would have come sooner, but I was in the shower. May I help you?"

His wet hair corroborated his story. Grateful for any help, I replied, "Yes, please, if you would accompany me inside, it would be much appreciated."

He came willingly. As we entered the house, I commented, "The thieves certainly chose the wrong house to rob. We don't have jewelry, money, or any valuables."

I had no idea how important that statement would become. Inside, I found everything dumped out and tossed around. We walked through littered documents, office supplies, files, books, mattresses, and drawers. Each room had been trashed. The glass in the French doors was broken, presumably how the thieves had entered. When we exited into the patio, I saw heavy ropes connected to massive iron hooks. Knotted bedspreads held small electrical appliances and anything else of resale value.

Our house like most residences in Paraguay had a high surrounding wall topped with barbed wire and implanted glass shards. Thin mattresses had been tossed over the wall separating our house from the house where my companion rented a room, presumably to protect the thieves from the barbed wire and glass. A ladder had been placed against the wall on the other side. The thieves had been clearly using the hooks and ropes to hoist their bedspread bundles of booty over the wall.

Chapter Forty-Two: Thieves!

The neighbor offered to drive around the block to see if he could catch the thieves with the goods they'd already hoisted over the wall. As he left, I thanked him profusely. Shortly after, Bill drove up. Stepping into what had an hour before been his tidy, organized office, he hugged me close and said, "Honey let's pray!"

Tight in his embrace, I rejoiced in his loving heart-talk to his heavenly Father. "Kind and gracious Lord, I thank you for protecting Hilda. Thank you that she is safe. Please give us wisdom to know what steps to take. Whoever these thieves are, please change their evil hearts. Once again, we commit ourselves and our home to you to be used for your honor and glory."

I'd always enjoyed looking up from my petite height to admire my husband's handsome six foot, four inch frame. But that day, I saw him not just as a physically large man but a spiritual giant of deep faith and sterling character. In the middle of our wrecked house, his first response was to give thanks to God that I was safe and that God was with us.

Two weeks later, neighbors knocked on our front door with a newspaper. They showed us a photo and accompanying news story. "This man in this photo is the one who planned the robbery of your house."

We immediately recognized our Brazilian neighbor. He'd been arrested by the police, and the news story reported that he was considered to be a long-term member of a Brazilian mafia with a lengthy criminal record of murders and robberies. It was now clear he'd arranged the team that came over the wall. I was typically gone from early morning until 12:30 p.m. teaching at the

Theological Institute, so he undoubtedly thought they had plenty of time to lift our belongings over the wall and through the night club, which was empty at that hour, then load them into a truck. When I'd come in from my walk, he'd jumped back over the wall and into the shower to give himself an alibi.

With his violent record, we were fortunate that he hadn't returned. I credit my casual comment that we kept no valuables in the house for that as he clearly decided our house wasn't worth the effort of a second visit. In all the months he'd lived next door, he must have heard the gospel many times through the Bible stories, singing, and prayers of our weekly outdoor children's Happy Hour. But instead of being convicted, he'd chosen to continue his evil lifestyle.

We now had even more reason to praise God for His protection on that day and for this man being removed from our neighborhood and off the streets for good.

Chapter Forty-Three

Another Adios

By 2000, God was showing Bill and me that our time in Paraguay was coming to an end. God had continued to work mightily in the twelve years we'd been there. Not only was the evangelical church exploding with growth, but there were more and more well-trained godly pastors and national church leadership, many of them graduates and students of the Theological Institute.

A single ministry newsletter we'd sent to our family and supporting friends a year prior gave just a handful of ways God was using our recent graduates. Marta directed a Bible study and feeding program for street children. Seratti was forming a Christian police network with the goal of seeing at least one believer in each police station. Alejandro was leading an evangelistic team in needy rural towns. Tito was the assistant pastor of a dynamic congregation of five thousand. Oscar was planting a new church in the small town of Itacurubi. Lourdes was leading Christian girls' clubs and drama teams. Pati served two thousand needy children in ChildCare (now ChildHope) schools, an AG-sponsored program that provides affordable Christian education to needy children across Latin America.

Another of our students had been part of a dangerous street gang in his teens. He'd contracted polio, which left him permanently confined to a wheelchair. Full of bitterness, he'd found temporary relief in alcohol. In 1981 when he was nineteen years old, someone shared the gospel with him. He gave his heart to Jesus and was instantly transformed. He began reading the Bible and shared his newly-found faith with members of his street gang.

He loved soccer, following one top team in particular. One day he asked the coach if he could share God's Word with the players. That following Sunday, he was given the opportunity to share before an important playoff game. But the team was more interested in knowing whether God had told him who would win the game. He responded, "If God wills, we will win."

They lost the game, and he wasn't invited back. But several years later, he was invited to be that team's chaplain, a position he held for more than six years. On Wednesdays and Fridays, he held a Bible study and prayed with the soccer players. On Sundays before each game, he encouraged the players with Scripture and prayer. At the same time, he studied for the ministry at the Theological Institute.

The testimonies of other dedicated Paraguayan Christians made us feel honored to be serving alongside them. One Asuncion church had issues with a disgruntled neighbor who tried to get all those living near the church to sign a petition forcing it to close. The troublemaker suddenly suffered a heart attack. Instead of rejoicing, the church leaders visited him in the intensive care unit, praying for him and donating blood. God healed him, and his entire family became part of that church.

On Valentine's Day, Bill was invited to speak at a large AG church in Asuncion. At the conclusion of his message, he encouraged husbands to express their love to their wives in a tangible way, suggesting flowers or perfume. A Christian businessman sitting in the congregation heard Bill's recommendation and felt impressed by God's Holy Spirit to respond.

Roberto was an importer of expensive European perfumes. He'd received a shipping container with his most recent order of perfume. But he'd discovered that the huge metal crate had been damaged in route. The perfume bottles were intact, but the ornate name-brand boxes were squashed and broken, making the perfume impossible to sell in its intended luxury market.

Meanwhile, our colleague and director of Paraguay's Teen Challenge ministry Dr. Rodney Hart had been praying with his team for God provide the urgent financial needs of their growing outreach in the Tacumbu prison and their rural rehabilitation camp site. Roberto donated the entire perfume shipment to Teen Challenge. For the following two years, former drug addicts and traffickers transformed by God's power sold these perfumes at greatly reduced prices at the entrances of supermarkets around Asuncion. The proceeds financed this expanding and effective drug-rehabilitation ministry.

There are far more stories we could tell that just will not fit in this book. But by late 2000, God had pressed upon Bill and me both that it was time to turn over directorship of the Theological Institute to the very capable Paraguayan Assemblies of God leadership. We accepted an invitation from the Costa Rican Assemblies of God to help once again in its Bible Institute and to organize a team to present the drama *Heaven's Gates* throughout that country.

As we packed up and prepared to leave, Bill and I were invited to share one last time with our Paraguayan Assemblies of God pastors and leaders. I shared some life lessons that as I termed it I'd "caught" rather than "been taught" from our dear Paraguayan friends.

They'd taught us *acceptance*. Though we were foreigners, they'd embraced us, sharing fellowship, meals, vacations, and jokes. When we struggled over a child's immature decisions thousands of miles away, they'd prayed with and for us as a family. They'd taught us that one doesn't have to be rich to show *generosity*, filling our home with gifts of food, plants, beautiful local crafts, and other gifts.

They'd taught us by example what *joyful sacrifice* was all about. Julio didn't even have a bed to sleep on, but insisted on making a mission faith promise. Ceferino walked four miles to the Theological Institute to give his bus fare to missions. Eunice gave up a good-paying job to serve fulltime co-directing the *Heaven's Gate* drama at one tenth the salary. Blanca had made her bicycle the neighborhood ambulance, balancing sick people on the back to take them to receive medical help.

They'd taught us the meaning of *fun and fellowship*. The Paraguayans didn't need a fancy program or expensive food and decorations. Simply being together sharing stories, jokes, and

Chapter Forty-Three: Another Adios

games made a party special. They'd also set an example of *respect*. When an older person entered a room, children and youth stood to greet them. They greeted adults respectfully as Sister Hilda or Brother Bill, not by their first names. The only "old folks" homes were nursing facilities for the critically ill or those without families. Children and grandchildren graciously cared for the aged.

And finally, the Paraguayan believers had taught us that a funeral could be a celebration when it was a homecoming into God's presence. No one-hour service as was typical in North America. During twenty-four-hour wakes, family and friends played guitars, mariachis sang about heaven, people gave testimonies and shared Scriptures. There were hugs and tears of joy as well as pain. The following day, family and friends walked with the casket all the way from their home to the cemetery.

Adios, beautiful Paraguay!

Chapter Forty-Four

Just the Way He Likes It!

Before moving back to Costa Rica, we spent some time on furlough in the United States. Phil and Karen were now living in Indianapolis, Indiana. While visiting them, we took their two daughters to the Indianapolis Zoo. We had parked and were getting out of our car when we saw a family group of children, parents, and grandparents excitedly greeting each other a few feet away.

"I've brought you something from Colombia," we overheard the patriarch of the family say.

The mention of Colombia, another South American country, was all it took for Bill to walk over and introduce himself. He asked the man, "What took you to Colombia?"

"My wife and I just returned from an exploratory trip there," the man responded. He introduced himself as David and his wife as Candy. "We will be going back with a group of Christian women from here in Indiana to paint and furnish a Bible Institute there. Candy takes a team to a different country each year."

"How interesting," Bill commented. "My wife Hilda and I are just transitioning from Paraguay, where we served in a Bible Institute, to Costa Rica, where we will be doing the same."

Now the other couple was equally intrigued. Candy asked, "So with what mission do you serve?"

"Assemblies of God World Missions," Hilda responded.

"What a coincidence!" Candy exclaimed. "My husband David is the secretary treasurer of the Indiana district of the Assemblies of God, and I am the director of women's ministries."

"Well, in the future, if you'd like to take a team to a beautiful country of warm, loving people, maybe you'll think of Costa Rica," I suggested.

We exchanged business cards and went our separate ways. But that out-of-the-blue meeting in a zoo parking lot proved to be just the beginning of a God-orchestrated plan. We returned to Costa Rica where we found that its culture, economy, and tourism had drastically changed in the twelve years we'd been gone. We were also thankful to see much growth from God-seeds planted years before. Former students were now leading growing congregations, serving their communities spiritually and practically.

A year later, I came across Candy's business card on my desk and contacted her through the email address given. "Hi, Candy. I'm the zoo lady you met by chance (divine appointment) at the Indianapolis zoo. There are urgent needs in Costa Rica, especially at the national Bible Institute. Would you consider blessing Costa Rica as you have other countries?"

Candy responded that she and her women's ministries committee would pray about the possibility. She later informed me they had decided to target Costa Rica for 2003. Candy and David flew down for an exploratory trip. At Candy's request, missionaries and national leaders compiled wish lists for various projects, which Candy in turn shared with the Indiana AG women's ministry leaders.

In November 2002, Candy invited me to the Indiana AG annual women's convention in Indianapolis. I watched humbled as women from many different places and backgrounds brought in their gifts for Costa Rica, including electrical appliances, linens, kitchen and bathroom items, and school supplies. Many had already sent cash offerings to purchase commercial kitchen appliances, mattresses, and other larger items.

On Monday morning, a huge shipping container rolled into the parking lot, where a wonderful team of volunteers braved the cold to pack it with a total of 564 boxes. Miraculously, everything fit in the container without space for a single additional box. Its contents were valued at over $130,000, including stoves, refrigerators, freezers, deep fryers, a hundred mattresses, thirty eight-foot tables, three hundred folding chairs, and on and on.

When the packing was done, we all joined hands and hearts in a large circle and thanked God who had inspired Candy to meet urgent needs through all of these precious, dedicated women. God protected that container even when it was mistakenly sent first to Panama, where it was thankfully intercepted and redirected to Costa Rica.

What a joy to see the expressions of those receiving each item as from God's gracious hand. The Bible Institute, Teen Challenge, Latin American Child Care, the language school, children's street evangelism and drama outreaches were all blessed.

Beyond these gifts, a total of 106 women from Indiana AG churches came in two-week stints to clean, repair, paint, and sew. Despite finding themselves in a different context, culture, and language, God united them to work in close harmony, recognizing they were part of an exciting divine plan. Their constant response when asked how they were doing became the group's motto: "This is just the way we like it!"

As our Costa Rican AG superintendent watched these women sing while painting up on high scaffolding, installing dry wall, sewing, hanging wall borders, and other tasks, he remarked, "Ladies, you have given us a great example. Now we want to follow your example by giving and working sacrificially for others. Thanks for coming!"

Our bus driver Jorge commented, "During twenty-six years of providing private bus service, I have never felt such kindness."

Adriana, the manager of the hotel where the visiting team was being housed, joined us for devotions at the worksite. Observing the gifts they'd brought and their hard work, she said, "I have never seen a group like this. They are so unlike our usual corporate executive guests. The hotel owner, cooks, receptionists, and I have all noticed how you express love and concern for us as individuals. I just can't believe all these expensive pieces of equipment were purchased through the giving of women who aren't even of wealthy backgrounds. I'll never be the same, and I thank God for you. My husband and I now want to give more of ourselves to God."

Was it worth the effort? Missionaries, nationals, hotel personnel, bus chauffeur, and 106 Indiana ladies together expressed, "We have given but have received more!"

Candy added their motto with one small change: "That's just the way He likes it!"

Chapter Forty-Five

Divine Interventions in Costa Rica

Arriving back in San Jose, Bill and I found a small, upstairs apartment to rent in a four-family apartment complex. We soon became close friends with AG missionaries John and Mary, who lived below us. John was a former Marine and a creative builder who could seemingly fix anything. Mary was a former hippy and gifted linguist. When they'd first become followers of Christ, God had called them to China. They immediately started learning Mandarin, but doors to serve in China were tightly closed.

Assemblies of God World Missions suggested they use their many skills in Latin America until Chinese visas became available. After finishing language acquisition, John did building projects while Mary taught English to Latin Americans preparing for international missions. In the evenings, they helped us greatly with presenting the drama *Heaven's Gates.*

One morning John excitedly shared that God had spoken to him through a dream, saying it was time to serve in China. Mary was disappointed as she'd come to love the Spanish culture, people, and language. But she joined her husband in obeying God's call.

Chapter Forty-Five: Divine Interventions in Costa Rica

John immediately communicated with our AG missions director. He responded, "This is amazing! I just heard today from our area director in Northern Asia that for the first time in recent history permission to build has been granted. We urgently need builders there!"

At the exact right time, God divinely provided a talented couple to respond to this need. John and Mary inspired us by their commitment to follow God's directions at all costs. Soon John was repairing dilapidated buildings and constructing coffee houses and playgrounds across this North Asian country while Mary taught English in a school. They brought joy everywhere they served.

We were also delighted to reestablish contact with former students of ours, Guillermo and Sandra, who were now married and in fulltime ministry. They had planted four churches and invited Bill and me to share with the newest church plant. Church members Alejandro and Laura had offered their adjoining tin-roofed lean-to so more neighbors could worship God. Now even that extended space had become too small to seat families anxious to grow spiritually. How rewarding it was for us to see the harvest of good seed planted years before!

Later in 2001, two of our three children and their families were able to visit us in San Jose. Our three children have always been grateful for their Costa Rican heritage, of which they have many great memories and lasting friendships with Costa Ricans and other missionary kids. We were able to stay in the rented house of furloughing colleagues, so there was plenty of room. We visited the beach and planned an open house for national friends from our kids' childhood and teen years.

From early morning until evening on the day of the open house, guests came by in a steady stream. The adults sat together inside, laughing and remembering childhood experiences. Their kids and our grandkids played happily together outside despite the language barrier. A cook-friend had prepared large quantities of *arroz con pollo* (chicken and rice), a traditional Costa Rican feast. I prepared a large cabbage salad and baked cream-filled chocolate cupcakes.

But by afternoon, all the cupcakes were gone. I wondered what dessert I could come up with for the remaining guests who were arriving. At that moment, I heard the landlord's voice calling out through the open front door. My heart sank since the house had been rented to a single couple and was now packed with not only our own large family but countless guests.

But the landlord was smiling as he laid a large, artistically wrapped tray on the kitchen table, saying, "Mr. and Mrs. Bradney, my wife makes German cakes during the Christmas season. She wanted to share one with you."

We thanked him profoundly, explaining that it arrived at a most appropriate time. We served his wife's delicious cake to the arriving guests, thanking God for His bakery blessing at a needed time.

That same year, I taught an evening missions class at the Bible Institute. I invited a Costa Rican single missionary named Olga to share her experiences serving in Panama. She'd planted the first evangelical church in a town called Punto Alegre. Sometime later,

Chapter Forty-Five: Divine Interventions in Costa Rica

she was visiting another town where she'd also planted a church when she fell into conversation with a local businessman.

"Where are you from?" he asked.

"From Punto Alegre," she responded.

"That town used to be a fun place," he commented. "The boats would come in, and the sailors and fishermen would enjoy having sex with the local girls, especially during carnival season. It was a drug traffic point from Colombia, and you could get any cheap drugs you wanted. Then some woman moved in, and the town has completely changed. No more fun or carnivals."

He had no idea he was speaking to the woman God had used to transform Punto Alegre and other communities. As Olga was sharing her experiences, a student named Tamira seated at the front of the class started crying. After the class, Olga and I prayed with Tamira. She asked if she could share during the next class.

Tamira shared that she was the only Christian in her family. When she was five years old, she was deeply impacted by a young woman who walked down the mountain path where she lived to attend a little evangelical church near Tamira's home. A staunch Catholic, Tamira's mother wouldn't allow Tamira to enter the evangelical church. But she'd secretly snuck in and listened to the young woman teach a Bible class to a group of children.

Tamira greatly admired the young woman from the way she dressed to her shoes. But above all, she was drawn to the joy and peace the young woman radiated. Right there silently in the class, she gave her heart to Jesus, wanting to be just like this woman and do what she did.

Years later, Tamira moved to San Jose to finish her university degree. By this time, she was attending an evangelical church and studying at the Bible Institute. God had called her to serve Muslims, and she'd even changed careers to become a physical therapist as a platform to reach Muslims. Listening to Olga share, Tamira realized that Olga was her childhood heroine who had led her to Christ in that children's class.

Finishing her story, Tamira told the class, "If God could use Olga at just twenty-four years old without regular financial support to plant churches in sinful towns without accessible roads, then He can use me!"

Tamira renewed her commitment to fulfil God's call to reach Muslims. That night as I returned home, I could hardly sleep reflecting on God's divine interventions.

One other divine intervention stands out from our second stint serving in Costa Rica. We had met Steffanie in Paraguay, where she worked at the American embassy. A Christian, she'd become interested in our ministry, keeping in touch with each new State Department posting, visiting us, and sending offerings for ministry projects. We hadn't seen her in some years when we received a check from her with a note in the memo line that read: "Give the Devil a Black Eye!"

We had to chuckle, not just at the image she evoked but because she couldn't possibly know we'd been facing seemingly insurmountable obstacles in trying to launch the gospel drama *Heaven's Gates* in Costa Rica. The computers at Customs had crashed so we couldn't complete the paperwork to get needed

Chapter Forty-Five: Divine Interventions in Costa Rica

equipment out of Customs. Nor had we budgeted the funds we were being told we'd have to pay for import duty. Time was running out, so the entire fifty-member cast had come together to pray and fast as well as rehearse with our *Heaven's Gates* leadership team. Steffanie's check arrived right at this critical time and was enough to pay the duty fees so that the equipment was released.

Meanwhile, Fernando, a local youth who helped in the drama, experienced problems bringing the equipment over the mountains from the port city where it had been shipped to San Jose. The truck broke down five times along the way, each time with a different problem. Hot, dirty, and exhausted, Fernando complained, *Why me, Lord?*

He suddenly realized he was fighting evil forces. As he resisted Satan, God encouraged him. He was even able to lead a man to Christ during one of his unwanted stops on the side of the road. A black eye for Satan indeed!

The needed equipment arrived ten minutes before the last practice. During the following three days, Fernando saw five of his family along with almost eight hundred others repent and commit their lives to Christ. Another black eye!

During Christmas 2002, more than five thousand Costa Ricans celebrated Jesus's birth in their hearts for the first time through having seen the drama *Heaven's Gates*. A secular TV news crew filmed parts of the drama and televised it on national news.

Chapter Forty-Six

Dream Fulfilled

Our children had often expressed, "Mom and Dad, you've invested decades serving in Latin America. Now it's our children's turn, your grandchildren, to have you close by and see more of you."

In 2003, we received a gracious invitation from Dr. Don Meyer, president of our alma mater, Eastern Bible Institute, renamed Valley Forge Christian College, (today it is University of Valley Forge) to serve as missionaries-in-residence. We would not only be helping prepare future global leaders in this academic setting near Philadelphia, PA, but would be able to enjoy more time with our own dear family, especially during academic holidays.

Bill and I left Costa Rica in July 2003 with one suitcase each and many emotional farewells. A house had been rented for us near the Valley Forge campus where we would start teaching in just two weeks. We rented a truck to take items we had in storage at our daughter's home as well as donated furnishings to our new home. Our son Phil also facilitated the purchase of a good used vehicle for us.

Unloading, we placed five coffee and end tables around our living area. Though they had originated from three different states, we were stunned to discover they all matched. We hung various pictures and other curios from Paraguay, India, and Costa Rica, made up our bed with donated linens and comforter, and hung window treatments.

When we'd finished, we looked around and realized that the donated furniture, souvenirs and pictures from the mission field, window treatments, and other second-hand items fit together as perfectly as though designed by an interior decorator. Our loving heavenly Father had provided for two of His children in such a practical yet beautiful way.

The Valley Forge General Hospital campus was near the infamous Valley Forge winter camp where George Washington and the Continental Army had suffered so brutally during the Revolutionary War, now a national historic site. Fittingly, the hospital served military veterans until it was closed by the Department of the Army General in 1974. In 1976, the extensive campus had become the new home of Eastern Bible Institute, renamed Valley Forge Christian College.

When walking through the deteriorated brick buildings to evaluate the possibilities of the property, the EBI administrative team discovered a post left written on a blackboard that read:

God protect these walls and these people. I hope that this place will soon again be a healer of the sick, teacher of knowledge, and haven for our defenders of peace. God bless!

That post proved prophetic as within the walls and grounds of VFCC precious young people both experienced healing and became God's healing hands to others. Expanding their knowledge of themselves, their major, and God's Word, they in turn became teachers to others. They responded to God's call for full-time missionary service all around today's challenging world, living and sharing His message of divine inner peace.

For the next sixteen years, Bill and I were privileged to witness God fulfilling the hope of whoever had left that scribbled chalk post behind on a blackboard. At first a huge learning curve challenged us. For more than three decades, we'd been teaching Spanish students in structured contexts. Now we needed to learn again American culture, idioms, academic rules, etc., all of which had changed greatly since we'd left for Costa Rica in 1970.

Dr. Meyer, his wife Evie, and other faculty greatly encouraged us and became close friends. We were excited to be teaching on this strategic campus where enrollment, prayer, missions giving, and outreaches were at an all-time high. Teams of dedicated students served Philadelphia's inner-city homeless along with Albanian, Korean, Hispanic, and countless other immigrant groups as well as many needing Christ from small towns to big cities. Bill and I were involved in student outreaches to Mexico, Honduras, Costa Rica, Peru, Paraguay, and Spain, as well as our local community.

Spending more time with our adult children and growing number of grandchildren was a very special benefit to living and serving in the United States. Our son Phil and his wife Karen had three children, Jessica, Rachel, and Blake, when they adopted two-year-old Joshua from a Russian orphanage. We cared for their three older children while Phil and Karen traveled to Russia to bring Joshua home.

During this time, I attended a parents' open house at Blake's Christian preschool. His teacher related how she'd been telling the class the story of Moses being rescued from the river by Pharaoh's daughter because God had a special plan for his life. She'd seen five-year-old Blake listening intently. The teacher asked the children to quietly pray about God's purpose for their own lives. She then asked, "Do any of you want to share with the class what you think God wants you to do?"

Blake's hand shot up. "Yes! God wants me to be a good brother to Joshua!"

Blake has continued to fulfill that priority since Joshua joined the Bradney family. The following winter school break, Bill and I visited Phil's family in Indiana. On our return, we took Joshua with us back to Pennsylvania to visit in our home and with Karen's mother, who lived nearby. Joshua was happily drawing and playing in the back seat of our car when a white-out blizzard swept in, making driving extremely hazardous.

We prayed fervently since treacherous ice had turned the interstate into a skating rink with large SUVs stuck in snow drifts and trailer trucks overturned. When a semi-trailer careened over the center island into our traffic lane just inches from our little Ford Taurus car, we knew we had to exit the highway. Zigzagging around stalled vehicles, we edged our way to an open exit and into an adjoining motel parking lot, where we were able to get the last unoccupied room.

For three days, we were stuck but safe in this motel room. Kind motel owners gave us lower rates and brought in food. Joshua, now an adult, still recalls how God provided a place for us to sleep, fun games, pillow fights, and many other good memories. We are so grateful it wasn't the ice that directed our car but God's divine protection.

As Joshua grew, we discovered that he like scores of orphans from over-crowded, under-staffed Russian and Eastern European orphanages didn't know how to process emotions or even how to cry. His orphanage had eighty children under the age of three. No matter how hungry, tired, wet, dirty, or sick they were, they quickly learned that crying would bring no response from caregivers. Like the other children, Joshua had unconsciously learned to mask his emotions and never cried even when hurting.

While we were teaching at VFCC, by then the University of Valley Forge, a teenaged Joshua accompanied us to a school concert. The chapel was crowded with students, visiting parents, and friends. We found seats and enjoyed the varied instrumental and choral arrangements, but above all we were keenly aware of God's sacred presence. Student worship leaders asked us to join them in song.

As Joshua sang, I noticed his eyes were closed and tears flowed down his cheeks. When the song time concluded, Joshua whispered, "Grandma, this is the first time I've ever cried!"

We hugged tightly, grateful for this holy moment

Bill and Hilda with grandchildren

Chapter Forty-Seven

More Divine Interventions

As always, hearing and witnessing the stories of God's divine interventions in our students' lives was one of our greatest delights and blessings. Milton from Peru had thought his dream of success and money would come true in the United States but found only loneliness, poverty, and emptiness. One day a Christian customer at the pizza franchise where Milton worked befriended him. Daniel shared the gospel, and Milton saw in Daniel the purpose, joy, and peace for which he longed. In time, Milton became an outstanding VFCC student and the leader of a growing multi-ethnic congregation.

During an academic spring break, we led a twenty-four-member student team to the huge metropolis of Mexico City for evangelistic outreach. Our hosts there rented a bus for the team's transportation. Witnessing the joy and peace reflected in our students, our chauffeur and his partner decided they were missing God's favor living together unmarried. So during our time there, they completed the civil process to legally marry.

I asked if we could celebrate their union under God. They were delighted, so we held a Christian wedding right there on the bus. We gave the newly married couple a Spanish Bible and bouquet of flowers. Bill read appropriate scriptures, encouraging them to walk with Jesus as husband and wife. That very next Sunday, the couple began attending a local evangelical church.

We met a slender blonde education major named Jessica our second year at VFCC. We'd encouraged the students to attend a three-day AG youth missions conference held in the mid-west for thousands of college students from all over North America. AG missionaries from various continents shared their ministries. Students were challenged to give a year to missions and pray about life-time missionary service. Burdened for those who hadn't heard God's Good News, Jessica responded at the altar, praying, "I won't leave this altar until You speak to me! I want to do Your will. Please reveal it to me!"

Long after other students had gone to bed, Jessica was still pouring out her heart to God. When the early morning cleaning team arrived, she remained at the altar, where God had burdened her heart for Africa. The following day, she visited the African exhibition, speaking with several ministry leaders serving there about educational needs in Africa.

On the last day of the missions event, she met a school principal from a war-torn African country. When Jessica filled out an application for that ministry, the principal excitedly exclaimed, "Your name is Jessica? When I was praying for this conference, God impressed on me that I would meet a Jessica who would bless our country. Now here you are! You are an answer to prayer, Jessica, and your gifts will be used to the maximum in our country!"

Jessica soon graduated with her teaching degree and in 2006 arrived in Somalia, where she served for three years before marrying a Swedish aid worker named Erik. For the next five years, they served together in both Kenya and Somalia. Then in October 2011, Jessica and a Danish colleague were traveling to a training event in southern Somalia when they were taken hostage by Somalian pirates.

For the next three months, they were held captive in one filthy desert encampment after another while the pirates negotiated for a demanded ransom for forty-five million dollars. Jessica suffered from a medical condition, and her health was deteriorating greatly. She worried that she might die out there and never return to her husband and family. The pirates couldn't even pronounce her name, making her feel even more alone.

Then one night there was a gunfire attack on the latest camp. Fearing for her life, Jessica tried to burrow into the sand to avoid the gunfire. Then she heard the most comforting sound—her name. "Jessica!"

The voice was clearly someone from her home country of the United States. She quickly discovered that the attack had come from an American special operations team, Navy SEAL Team Six. Her heavenly Father who knew her name and had never left her had answered her prayers. The SEAL team soon escorted Jessica and her Danish colleague to a nearby combat helicopter, which flew them to freedom and their waiting families.

Jessica's ninety-three-day ordeal and rescue captured headlines around the world as she gave thanks to God, President Obama, and

Chapter Forty-Seven: More Divine Interventions

the courageous Navy SEAL team that had rescued her. She and her husband Eric returned to the United States, where they later had a son. Her full story can be read in her memoir *Impossible Odds*.

These were just a few of the God interventions we were privileged to witness while serving at Valley Forge Christian College. In just one ministry newsletter written in late 2012, we shared of God's amazing grace in the lives of the following students.

Nicole was made whole from painful abuse after attending a class where she received and offered forgiveness. Bill and I received a three-page handwritten letter thanking God for healing her emotional wounds. She now serves others.

Aubrey invited artists to painting parties, sold the art at weekend events, then gave the proceeds to rescue girls from human trafficking in India. Rachel was preparing to serve in the Democratic Republic of Congo, creating health curriculum for schools to help reduce that country's epidemic-level HIV virus. Four students were heading to Cairo, Egypt, to learn Arabic culture and language so as to creatively live and share the good news among unreached people groups in the Middle East. Students packed 174 Operation Christmas Child shoe boxes for needy children around the world. Groups of students were serving victims of Hurricane Sandy, the deadliest storm of the 2012 Atlantic hurricane season.

And that was just one newsletter. As in Costa Rica and Paraguay, the stories of our students serving God and being touched by God could go on and on.

Missions Convention at Valley Forge Christian College.

Hilda playing Paraguayan harp for Children.

Chapter Forty-Eight

Aussie Adventure

Our State Department friend Stephanie who'd worked in the U.S. embassy in Paraguay continued to bless us, not just giving to many mission projects but in 2013 providing funds for an unspoken dream I'd had for decades to revisit my childhood home in Australia and introduce Bill to that country and friends there.

Our hosts during our trip were Steffan Lowe and his sister Erin. The Lowes were an Anglo-Indian family my parents had led to Christ in Calcutta, India. We had reconnected after they immigrated to Melbourne, Australia, and visited the family many times as children in Australia. With the Lowes, we visited Phillip Island Nature Park, where we enjoyed the penguins, kangaroos, and koalas.

We also reconnected with Chris and Erica Grace, whom we'd first met during our 1986-87 furlough when Chris studied with my husband in Assemblies of God Theological Seminary post-graduate courses. Always adventurous, Chris had left his hometown of Sydney, Australia, to travel the world. He'd been working with French geologists in the Peruvian jungle when he contracted hepatitis. An elderly American missionary couple offered him hospitality while he recuperated.

Chapter Forty-Eight: Aussie Adventure

One night over dinner, Chris was sharing his travel experiences when his host commented with discernment, "Chris, you've been in many places and done many things. But, son, you are still searching!"

Chris didn't care for the comment since he'd always thought he had it all together. But later when he was alone, he prayed, *God, if what I've heard about You tonight is true, show me.*

God's Spirit powerfully convicted Chris, and he immediately fell to his knees weeping. He'd grown up in the Christian faith, and he now felt like the prodigal son returning to his spiritual home. Wanting to grow spiritually, he'd studied at the AG Theological Institute in Asuncion where Bill and I later taught. While there, Chris met Erica, the daughter of AG missionaries serving in Bolivia. They were married and became AG missionaries, serving six years in Paraguay, five in Bolivia, and nine in Chile.

At the time we met Chris and Eric in Springfield, their family was facing a major crisis. Their six-year-old son Andrew was losing his sight from a cerebral virus that had atrophied the optic nerve. He'd been treated by eye specialists in Australia, Chile, and the United States, but his eyes continued to deteriorate. By kindergarten, Andrew couldn't see writing on the blackboard even when sitting in the front row of his classroom.

That Easter 1987, I took Andrew and our oldest grandson Bobby, Ruth's son, to an egg hunt in a local park. The whistle blew, and the children dashed to gather eggs. All except Andrew, who just stood watching. He couldn't see the eggs. On hands and knees, I gathered some for him.

Chris shared Andrew's need in the seminary chapel. The Grace family's return to serve in Chile was in jeopardy as Andrew would need specialized schooling. A group of students fasted and prayed, asking God to touch Andrew's eyes. A few days later, a classmate told Chris he'd felt God telling him to give Chris a vial of oil, saying, "Anoint your son with this for seven days, and God will heal him."

Andrew's parents had anointed his eyes and prayed for healing many times. But once again, they did so, anointing and praying with him each night before bed. On the eighth morning, they awoke to delighted shouts. "I can see them! I can see them!"

Springing out of bed, Chris and Erica found Andrew looking out the front window, delighted to finally see the squirrels he'd heard his parents and brothers describe. Erica likes to believe that God told the squirrels to put on a show just for Andrew. That day, Andrew not only received healing of his eyes but also received Jesus into his heart. Eye surgeons confirmed the miracle, and Andrew's healing became an important platform to tell Chileans of God's divine intervention in their little son.

Years later, I called the Grace family while ministering at a national women's convention in Chile and spoke with Andrew. He praised God that his eyes were still totally fine. Now all these decades later, we reconnected in a Melbourne café over English scones with strawberry jam and Devonshire cream and caught up on their ministry.

After their service in Chile, Chris and Erica been invited to coordinate the missions department of the Assemblies of God in Chris's home country of Australia. Later, Erica began producing

Chapter Forty-Eight: Aussie Adventure

family programming for HCJB Christian radio based in Quito, Ecuador, while her husband pastored a local Australian church. When we met them at that Melbourne café, Erica's radio success had led to writing books and giving national TV family seminars across Australia.

We traveled to Adelaide, South Australia, as well where we fellowshipped with the Pitman family, dear childhood friends I'd grown up with in the church my parents pastored there. We also reconnected with the Evans family, whose parents Tom and Stella had served with my parents in both India and later in the Adelaide church. Andrew Evans had served as superintendent of the Assemblies of God in Australia. In 2002, he'd co-founded the conservative political party The Family First and had won a seat in South Australia's legislative council.

What a joy it was to trace our two families' very distinct but spiritually fruitful journeys from where our parents had first met serving God together in India. Altogether, it was a wonderful trip of reconnecting and making new memories in my childhood home of Australia, and I will never be able to thank sweet Stephanie enough for making it possible.

Epilogue

Not Retired But Retreaded

As Bill and I approached our eighties, we realized it was time to transition from structured teaching to a less demanding life-style, especially when we reviewed our calendar and realized we were now attending more funerals than weddings. Our last official year of teaching at the University of Valley Forge was 2018. God provided for us a lovely senior community called Garden Spot Village in Lancaster County, Pennsylvania.

One day as Bill sat in our cottage sunroom, he talked candidly with God. "Lord, we don't deserve such a lovely cottage with such a beautiful view overlooking manicured lawns, roses, birds, squirrels, and rabbits."

He seemed to hear God whisper lovingly, "You have lived long enough behind barred windows and doors, high walls, barbed wire, and glass shards while serving Me in Latin America. This beautiful spot where you can view My handiwork is My divine hug to you!"

From that moment, Bill accepted and thanked God for this gracious gift. Today, society may call us retired. I believe God would call us retreaded as we continue to serve Him in any way we can, though our service and location has transitioned from university students to adults and seniors. I'm blessed in a limited way to serve

Epilogue: Not Retired But Retreaded

our growing local church congregation, share leadership in several groups, and volunteer with Bill in our community.

In 2019, Bill and I traveled with my daughter Ruth, son Phil, and grandson Josh to visit former neighbors, friends, colleagues, students-now-pastors in Costa Rica where we'd served for a total of almost twenty years. The national church association welcomed us with a traditional feast and open house on the Bible Institute campus. What a fiesta to see and hear how former students are reaching this generation in new and effective ways. Tears, laughs, hugs, gifts, and stories filled each day. We saw children of former neighbors who had accepted Christ in our home now loving and serving God.

We were grateful and blessed to have taken this trip as the 2020 global Covid-19 pandemic pushed the pause button on travel. Millions have experienced death, pain, separation, job loss, fear, and isolation during this pandemic. Thankfully, Bill and I have kept well, learned more computer skills to connect electronically, and I was able to dedicate this time to document and share these stories.

One of my special joys is to invite guests around our dining-room table to share stories. Recently, we had the privilege of personally meeting three more precious servants of God who shared their stories of being greatly impacted by my dad during his final years—Rev. Sam Smucker, founder of the Lancaster, PA, Worship Center, international speaker and teacher Andrew Taylor, and international evangelist and author Christopher Alam. Seeds Dad sowed in their lives have flourished over many decades, continuing to bring hope to thousands around the world.

Bill and I have now completed more than sixty years of married life. In June 1961 when we knelt at an altar during our wedding ceremony, we had no idea of where, how, or when God would confirm His words spoken through my dad: "If you are faithful to the Lord, He will use you in a unique way to bless multitudes in missions."

By His grace, Bill and I have seen this prophecy fulfilled. We have witnessed God do far more than we could ever imagine or guess or request in our wildest dreams as God promised His followers through the apostle Paul.

> Now to Him who is able to [carry out His purpose and] do superabundantly more than all that we dare ask or think [infinitely beyond our greatest prayers, hopes, or dreams], according to His power that is at work within us. (Ephesians 3:20, AMP)

As we celebrate sixty fruitful and fulfilling years of marriage and team service, Bill and I truly feel we are the happiest, most fulfilled couple in the world. My faithful, loving, and supportive husband has constantly encouraged and enabled me to continue studying, accept ministry invitations, and enjoy hobbies.

That includes experienced and collecting the stories of God's divine intervention until God closes my earthly book. I look forward by God's grace to the eternal day when He opens His Book of Life and I hear Him call my name. I anticipate thanking and worshipping Jesus who planned my little life. I will embrace loved ones and friends to hear the rest of their stories.

I anticipate seeing you there and hearing your story also

Not Retired but Retreaded.
Bill and Hilda at Garden Spot.

About the Author

Born in India to British missionaries Harold and Hilda Groves, author, professor, conference speaker, and missions veteran Hilda Bradney served with her husband Bill with the Assemblies of God for more than fifty years, including the United States, Costa Rica, and Paraguay, and as chair and adjunct professor of the University of Valley Forge's Department of Intercultural Studies. Now "retreaded" in Lancaster County, PA, the Bradneys continue serving God in their local community and enjoy spending time with their three children and spouses, eight grandchildren and four great grandchildren.

You can reach the author at **billhilbradney@gmail.com**.

Made in the USA
Middletown, DE
03 August 2024